THE ROCK AND ROLL STORY

From the Sounds of Rebellion to an American Art Form

CHARLES T. BROWN

Saginaw Valley State College

PRENTICE-HALL, INC., Englewood Cliffs, New Jersey 07632

Library of Congress Cataloging in Publication Data

BROWN, CHARLES T.
  The rock and roll story.

  Bibliography: p.
  Includes index.
  1. Rock music—History and criticism.   I. Title.
ML3534.B77 1983   784.5′4′009   83-10996
ISBN 0-13-782227-8

Editorial/production supervision and
    interior design: Patricia V. Amoroso
Cover design: Diane Saxe
Manufacturing buyer: Raymond Keating

©1983 by Prentice-Hall, Inc., Englewood Cliffs, New Jersey 07632

*All rights reserved. No part of this book may be
reproduced, in any form or by any means,
without permission in writing from the publisher.*

Printed in the United States of America

10 9 8 7 6 5 4 3 2 1

ISBN 0-13-782227-8

PRENTICE-HALL INTERNATIONAL, INC., *London*
PRENTICE-HALL OF AUSTRALIA PTY. LIMITED, *Sydney*
EDITORA PRENTICE-HALL DO BRASIL, LTDA., *Rio De Janeiro*
PRENTICE-HALL CANADA INC., *Toronto*
PRENTICE-HALL OF INDIA PRIVATE LIMITED, *New Delhi*
PRENTICE-HALL OF JAPAN, INC., *Tokyo*
PRENTICE-HALL OF SOUTHEAST ASIA PTE. LTD., *Singapore*
WHITEHALL BOOKS LIMITED, *Wellington, New Zealand*

CONTENTS

Preface *iv*

1 ROOTS OF ROCK *1*

2 EARLY ROCK—PRE-BILL HALEY *16*

3 BILL HALEY AND THE COMETS *24*

4 ELVIS PRESLEY *32*

5 BROADENING OF THE STYLE *51*

6 ATTITUDES OF THE 1960s *77*

7 THE BEATLES *81*

8 CALIFORNIA—NORTH AND SOUTH *95*

9 ATTITUDES OF THE 1970s *108*

10 TECHNOLOGY AND ELECTRONICS *112*

11 ENGLISH ROCK *118*

12 FOLK AND ECLECTIC ROCK *131*

13 JAZZ-ROCK, FUNK, AND DISCO *147*

14 PUNK AND NEW WAVE *169*

15 ROCK HALL OF FAME *182*

Discography *196*

Bibliography *200*

Index *202*

PREFACE

The Rock and Roll Story: From the Sounds of Rebellion to An American Art Form provides a complete history of rock and roll from its beginnings through the present. It is not an encyclopedia, nor does it include every rock musician who ever existed, but it does cover all the major movements and includes representatives of each style. It was written for the general public in a non-technical style so that the importance of this art form might be more fully understood. Although it is a book primarily about music, it certainly gives credit to the social impact of rock and roll and attempts to illustrate the relationship between culture and art.

I would like to thank my friends and colleagues listed in *The Art of Rock and Roll* for their contribution to my life, my wife for giving me time to work on this version of the rock and roll story, and my students who continue to encourage me. Also, I would thank Bud Therien and Jean Wachter at Prentice-Hall. With this book, I will have accomplished my goal of writing a book which functions for both academicians and the general public, as it has always been my belief that educators and the public ought to work together.

CHARLES T. BROWN

CHAPTER ONE

Roots of Rock

INTRODUCTION

Chapters One and Two deal with the roots of rock and the pre-Bill Haley period and are very important in telling the rock story. I have attempted to outline the basic forms that ultimately led to rock and roll; since rock is still influenced by its roots, one should certainly know about what happened before 1951. However, some readers might want to skip this information and start with Chapter Three; that's where the real stuff begins.

SLAVE MUSIC

Although we might properly term this section the history of African music in the United States, we actually begin with a discussion of slave music, because that is exactly what it was. Black people were forced to come to the United States, this alienating them from the environment or bringing about forced acculturation (cultural adaptation). The difference between free acculturation of a race or society and forced acculturation is quite significant; we must first recognize that Africans had little choice in their environment and free interchange with white society was not always possible.

The slave routes brought Africans to the New World through various ports, primarily in the southern United States, the Caribbean, and several places in Latin America. The slaves brought directly to the northern part of the United States traveled a different cultural path than those brought through the Caribbean. The kinds of music which developed from different cultural experiences is a study in itself (the bibliography at the end of the book provides excellent source material on this subject).

Most of the slaves imported to the New World came from West Africa, which brought about some continuity in the basic tribal experiences of the acculturation process. We will examine some of the kinds of music which were staples of the slaves and which were carried over into the nineteenth-century antecedents of the blues, as it influenced early jazz and later, rock and roll. In passing, it would be interesting to trace the influence of tribal roots in popular music in other American cultures, such as Brazilian cult and popular music (see the bibliography).

The first slaves were brought to the United States in the early seventeenth century, and it is important to understand that they were Africans and not Americans at all. As Western Africans, they would go through a long process before they became what we can call black Americans, or Afro-Americans (see LeRoi Jones, *Blues People*[1]). Jones, or Imamu Amiri Baraka, as he prefers to be called, traces the process of becoming Afro-American in a most convincing way. He points out that the original black slaves did not see themselves as Americans, but rather as captives. From this perspective, they did not immediately begin the process of free acculturation.

The original slaves viewed themselves as alien in this foreign land and believed that they would be returning to Africa. Also, they had to perform certain tasks on a schedule established by those in power. They did not give up their language, their view of the universe, or any of their customs (except those which were eliminated through punishment). There are analogies with other

---

[1] LeRoi Jones, *Blues People* (New York: William Morrow, 1967).

groups brought to the United States (such as the Orientals brought to build the railroad in the nineteenth century), but these are weak at best. The Indians of Latin America (most particularly Mexico) were acculturated rather freely, but they were the native population. Africans were alien in the land, they were not acculturated freely, and their roots were thousands of miles away.

In some sense, the most significant way of showing the slow process of acculturation for Africans would be through their use of language. Only when they began to tell their life stories in some form of English would they become truly Afro-American. Slave tradition relied heavily on African languages, or more properly, the people spoke two languages. Everything of substance was said in an African dialect; English was used for less substantive things, but also for survival.

Secular Tradition

The process of change in musical tradition for African slaves began quite early in the United States, primarily because they were spread out somewhat more thinly here than in other parts of the New World. Although there was a continuation of pure African traditions, the slow process of acculturation began as soon as there were American-born slaves, and that change was most apparent in secular music.

The only place where African slaves really saw themselves as part of this alien land was through the work they were forced to perform. And although the work was performed for different reasons and with weak motivation, it was done in a manner similar to that which would have been used in a tribal setting. As Africans quite naturally sang to help in the process of work, this became the focal point for change in their musical culture.

It is important to understand at this point that Africans do not necessarily recognize music as an art form, separate from life in general. To them, music is a part of living, and aside from certain religious events, it is not a separate experience. It is done in conjunction with life — with work and with daily activity. We are not trying to conjure up the image of the happy slave singing while enjoying hard work in the field, because this was not the case. There was a tremendous amount of misery involved in this forced labor. However, the fact that slaves did sing is true, although they sang because it helped them accomplish the work and avoid the misery about which we just spoke. Although their motivation for working in a tribal situation might have been stronger, hard work was necessary here, and their culture had trained them to sing while they were doing it. Later discussions of the blues will rely heavily on the patterns set up in work songs and the message of misery in the lives of black people, whether African or Afro-American.

The similarities of certain life experiences are the cornerstone of acculturation. The reason that some acculturation first took place in secular music is directly linked to the similarities between the secular experience (that is, work) in both Africa and the New World. Because of the massive dissimilarity between religious experiences (the African religious system was very different from those in this country), acculturation within religious music and traditions would occur much later.

Work songs were basically chants, first in African languages and then in English with African words thrown in. *Chants* are simple phrases that are repeated over and over, and the phrases are usually quite short. They are very rhythmic in that they usually have a short melodic phrase (three or four notes) and a reiterative rhythmic pattern. For example, "Song of the Volga Boat Man" is a work song, although it is quite different from African ones. Many children's songs have aspects of work songs, as do the chants of cheerleaders at football games. There are many fine sources for work songs of African slaves, and although certain characteristics survive in the blues, the actual rhythms or pitches of these early predecessors are pretty far from rock and roll.

A trait of early African work songs that is significant for later developments is the scale, or the melodies. The songs usually had three to five different notes, and the scale was not a Western one by any sense of the word. It normally contained a flatted third degree, giving it a sense of plaintiveness. The important point for us is that the scale degrees used in the melody later appear in what we will call the blues scale. These songs were quite simple, which should not be taken as a criticism of African music. The fact is, obviously, that work songs were sung during work, and it is probably unfair to expect Italian arias from people who are digging trenches.

It has been fairly well established that the music was performed mainly in unison, with everyone singing the same melody. However, there was a leader who sang one phrase, with the entire group responding to him or her. This *call-and-response* pattern is definitively African and has been retained in the blues tradition and in gospel music. Leaders, or *callers*, were very important in slave society, which is a direct implantation of the social structure of the tribe. The call-and-response pattern is the most often mentioned characteristic of African roots in black music in general.

Another type of secular music practiced quite far back in the history of slave music was the field holler. A *field holler*, or *cry*, was simply a message which was supposed to travel some distance. It could be a name, a simple command, or an expression of emotion, and it was usually voiced in an African dialect, which the white slave owners could not understand. As usual, it was functional, although occasionally it took on another meaning. It was short, sung in unison or by one person, and was rhythmically simple. Special characteristics of a field holler, which will be significant in our later discussion of blues style, are as follows:

1. It often used bending of notes to produce a sad or pushing feel to the melodic pattern.
2. It often used slides between notes, or drop-offs (the pitch is held and then is slid downward over a wide range).
3. It was usually more complex at the beginning and ended with a long, held note.

Field hollers established many of the patterns which would later become staples of early blues.

Religious Music

As previously stated, acculturated religious music occurred much later in the history of the slaves because there was such a massive difference between African religious concepts and the philosophy of Protestantism as it was practiced by whites in the United States. Generally speaking, African religions are animistic or naturalistic, in that they are polytheistic (worship many gods) and each god generally corresponds to some phenomenon in nature (water, fire, animal spirits, and so on). The *Loa*, or natural objects which have power or spirit in them, each deserve respect and appropriate rituals to appease or satisfy their needs. This kind of system does not correspond very well to anything contained in the kind of Puritan Protestantism of colonial America. Interestingly enough, there are significant parallels between Roman Catholicism and animistic religions which were used quite effectively in places like Mexico. However, there was no parallel in the United States, and our Puritan forefathers probably would not have used them even had they existed.

By virtue of this disparity, there was little way in which black people could be woven into the fabric of religious experience, and for a few centuries they were left on the outside as heathens. There were, of course, early attempts to convert American-born slaves by taking them away from their parents and raising them as Christians, but the differences in culture were so vast that this activity had little influence in creating a black Christianity.

However, like everything else in the slave's environment, white religious music became influential by the end of the eighteenth century, by which time the idea of returning to Africa must certainly have been waning in the blacks' view of reality. By 1780 or so, Christianity had a firm hold in the slave community, and its practice was occurring at the same time as that of certain African traditions, although later these would be dropped. However, there was at least one notable difference between the black-oriented Christian service and a comparable white service — the *spiritual*. Most common sources indicate that the spiritual was essentially a Christian hymn with a strong rhythmic beat imposed on it, in the singing style and in the accompaniment.

Although the previously discussed secular style had little influence from whites, the religious style of Protestant slaves most certainly was influenced by European tradition. Interestingly, there was an easing of Puritan values around the turn of the century, and certain taboos against emotion in religious experience were beginning to be thought of as old-fashioned. The beginning of the nineteenth century saw many changes in the United States, and certainly the move toward expressiveness was most significant from a cultural point of view. In other words, the philosophy of white religious experience was shifting to the point where certain aspects of the black experience could be consistent. Therefore, free acculturation was finally possible, even though the *Emancipation Proclamation* was still quite a few years off.

The spiritual was basically a Protestant hymn, with even phrases and standard European structure (for an explanation of structure, see the following section on the blues). What were added to make it a black experience were the rhythm of work songs and the call-and-response pattern of African tribal music. Instead of everyone singing the song straight through, the minister would sing one phrase, which would either be imitated by the congregation or followed by another phrase sung by the congregation. The singing was still in unison, without harmony. Hand-clapping and foot-stomping accentuated the rhythmic feel of the composition. The piano player would also add rhythmic figures in back of the singing. The result was a rhythmically alive composition, which made for a very different kind of performance than that in white churches. This free adaptation of a white style probably caused the growth of black Protestant sects, particularly in the South.

Gospel music (the religious blues) is a direct descendent of these spirituals; and at least the style of performance can be considered a direct antecedent to both jazz and rock and roll, although these are secular traditions. The separation between secular and sacred is usually quite thin; although it exists quite clearly in black attitudes toward music, both historically and in the present, there are many stylistic traits which are shared by both.

VAUDEVILLE

The significance of this particular form of entertainment is normally left out of a discussion of early sources of jazz because it is such a potpourri of musical styles. Vaudeville loosely defines the music and entertainment of traveling shows of people, somewhat like county fairs. A vaudeville show could consist of everything from plays, musicals, and boxing matches to full-scale concerts (like that of the Germania Orchestra of the 1850s). When vaudeville performances were musical, they were primarily symphonic, or they consisted of just folk songs. However, from this very important tradition came the minstrel show, which was an insulting comment on the black population. However, it was entertainment, and as such it was important to both small towns and large cities.

The important point for us is that vaudeville provided the first opportunity for folk songs (some of which contained black themes) to be institutionalized (sort of like the recording industry without records). Many of the traditions of vaudeville would be used later in black vaudeville circles, which fostered boogie-woogie, ragtime, Dixieland, and what will later be defined as urban blues.

Although vaudeville is less important as a source for jazz and rock, it is highly significant for performances, that is, the style of presenting music as a live experience. Without vaudeville, these popular musical forms might have remained regional arts, or even more, styles of one town. Vaudeville produced the first means for mass communication.

EARLY JAZZ FORMS

In this section, we will discuss some early jazz forms (as they are commonly defined), with the purpose of showing that they are really part of the development of rock and roll as an extension of jazz development. Most of these forms resulted from relatively free acculturation of black and European styles, although this statement may be debatable.

Cakewalk

Many of the early black minstrel shows (that is, minstrel shows in which the performers were black) were parodies of the minstrel shows first started by whites. White vaudeville performers would put on blackface (shoe polish or coal soot) and imitate black people. This imitation was later reimitated by black performers (even to the extent of using blackface). One very important part of the early development of black performing style was that blacks were constantly putting on their audiences — either laughing at themselves or at the whites who imitated them.

The cakewalk was an adaptation of a dance, but done in a square. People walked around the square and made flourishing movements as they turned the corners. This dance was traditional at church socials and is still performed in white tradition in parts of the Midwest. Black tradition developed a dance step in the form of a cakewalk, but its intention was to parody the stiff way in which whites walked and danced. As a parody it was successful in black circles and was probably the first truly Afro-American dance step. It enjoyed success on the scale of the twist, and it was danced by blacks and imitated by whites.

Ragtime

Ragtime was a piano style, developed around the turn of the century, whose significance to the history of jazz is well accepted. (Its history is well documented in source material in the bibliography.) It is clearly a black art form with definite European influence.

Ragtime is composed music, although it originated in oral or unwritten tradition. It usually has four main themes, which are divided into four sections of music equal in length. The general style and sound of the music are quite complex. Ragtime has the following features:

1. a left hand based on chords, which are broken up differently on each beat (commonly in a four-beat phrase)
2. a melodic right hand with complex figuration
3. uneven accenting between the two hands (syncopation).

Next to the black-oriented songs of Stephen Foster in the mid-nineteenth century, ragtime was the most published music from a black tradition until the 1940s. Although most of the black composers who played ragtime made little money from it, it was mass communication for both blacks and whites.

European influence is obvious in the sound of the music, the structure of the composition, and simply the fact that it is composed. Black influence can be heard in the rhythmic patterns (the syncopation) and in the swing (from the spiritual, discussed earlier). Ragtime is one of the best examples of an acculturated art form we could find. Scott Joplin and others clearly put together the influences of the European tradition with the black American experience. The result is not just European music; it is Afro-American music.

Stride

Stride is a style of playing the piano. James Johnson (considered to be the father of stride piano[2]), Willie "The Lion" Smith, and Thomas "Fats" Waller were early exponents of this particular style. Some later pianists who played stride piano (at least at times) were Art Tatum, Oscar Peterson, Duke

---

[2]Paul Tanner and Maurice Gerow, *A Study of Jazz*, 4th ed. (Dubuque, Iowa: W. C. Brown, 1981), pp. 59–62.

Ellington, and Count Basie. Stride piano has influenced many piano players, some of whom still play it today.

Stride is a direct outgrowth of ragtime, in that it uses a basic rag (or ragtime melody) as the foundation for improvisation. *Improvisation* is the act of making up additional music, based on some theme or some part of an original theme. Ragtime contains little improvisation, although free improvisation of thematic material is a staple that black musicians brought from tribal music. Stride piano, as an extension of ragtime, reintroduces the element of improvisation as the virtuosity (or technical ability) of the pianist becomes greater.

Stride is based on a concept of theme and variations — the pianist plays the basic theme (the rag melody) and then does one or more variations on it (improvisations). Stride piano is faster than ragtime in tempo, more flamboyant, and simply more intense in feeling. As the stride piano style developed, musicians used any theme available — from pop music, Dixieland, or the blues — and stride piano players became parts of instrumental ensembles (later as leaders of big bands, like Ellington or Basie). Jelly Roll Morton is the best example of a flamboyant solo stride pianist who later put together a full band (Dixieland in his case). Stride was probably the most important style for a pianist until the 1940s.

Dixieland

Dixieland is very easy to define in general terms, although a definitive definition would take another book (and then some people would argue with it). Dixieland is basically a musical style that developed in New Orleans in the first twenty years of the twentieth century and then moved to other cities in the United States, where it developed styles with noticeable differences. It is basically an instrumental style, requiring more than one instrument.

The standard Dixieland band of the early twentieth century in New Orleans contained a trumpet (cornet), clarinet, trombone, banjo, tuba, and drums. This was an instrumentation drawn from street bands or marching bands. The rhythm section, consisting of banjo, tuba, and drums, was the rhythm section of the street band (no piano was used until ragtime and Dixieland combined). The cornet played the melody, the clarinet a countermelody, and the trombone an elaborated bass line. Each of the melody instruments played solos in the variations which followed the presentation of the main melody.

The standard form of Dixieland was theme and variations, the melody being presented first and then the solos by the different melody instruments (backed up by the rhythm section). The melody was presented again for a conclusion. Although Dixieland may not be too significant in the history of rock and roll, some of the techniques of the solos can be heard in the evolution of rock. The important point is that it solidified the concept of a rhythm section that provided the background for the melody.

The rhythm section eventually substituted a piano for the banjo, substituted a string bass for the tuba, and increased the role of the drummer to provide true rhythmic interest (at first all three rhythm instruments played on every beat). The expansion of the role of the rhythm section and the resulting complexity of its intermixing is a significant example of what happens in rock and roll. Therefore, Dixieland is important to know about, both as a part of the development of jazz and as a model for rock and roll.

Boogie-Woogie

Boogie-woogie is another piano style which began sometime in the mid- to late 1920s. It is a very interesting style of playing because it has some similarities to stride piano in its intensity, but since it is somewhat more precise, it is easier to define.

Boogie-woogie was a black style associated with a circuit of black musicians who traveled from town to town to play for parties, often "rent" parties, where the musician would play for people who needed rent money. *Boogie* is a term derived from *bogey*, meaning spirit. *Woogie* is the name of the pieces of wood which tie together railroad tracks. Since many of the boogie-woogie piano players rode the trains (usually under the train), they were closely associated with the railroad ties. The clicking sound of the train can be heard in the long-short rhythmic pattern of boogie-woogie.[3]

In boogie-woogie the left hand plays a set pattern on the piano (usually with a feel of eight beats to the measure) and the right hand plays short melodic figures (sometimes called *riffs*). This is a form of theme and variations and is usually based on the blues progression, in twelve-measure phrases. It is freely improvised music, like stride piano, and many of its exponents have had major influence, although they made very little money from playing it. Boogie-woogie is the first obvious influence for rock and roll, and its patterns can be clearly heard in 1950s rock.

THE BLUES

The Pattern — Blues Progression

We have avoided using standard musical notation, but we must now define a musical scale in order to teach the blues progression. We will deal mainly with the underlying structure of the blues rather than the complexity of its possible variations. The following technique will teach a simple blues progression. If the reader wishes to go further, many fine publications on the blues are listed in the Bibliography.

A musical scale is a set of notes leading from one to another. For our purposes we will use the major scale of Western music, based on the following notes: C, D, E, F, G, A, B, C. This is one octave and can be counted in both ascending form (going up) and descending form (going down). A simple example of the latter is the song "Joy to the World," that is, the traditional form, not the rock song.

---

[3]Milton Stewart, "Polyrhythm and its Role in the Development of Structure in Boogie Woogie," presented at the National Association of Jazz Educator's Convention, Jan. 14-17, St. Louis, 1981.

```
Joy to the world the Lord is come.
 C   B  A  G  F  E  D  C
 8   7  6  5  4  3  2  1
```

There are very few songs that use a complete major scale in the opening eight notes, but "Joy to the World" is one of them. You will notice that we are talking about the melody without considering how long each of the notes is held. If we have not understood what a melody is yet, here is an example. The pitches themselves, without the words, form a melody, in this case a descending major scale.

The letters represent the notes as they could be played on a guitar or a piano. The numbers represent the scale degrees, which could be used to describe the different pitches in the scale and the relationships among them.

After we have mastered the idea of this scale and can see that the notes do have relationships with each other, we can begin to explain what a progression of notes is and how the blues should be understood. We will be using a standard explanation of the blues, although there are many variants. For our purposes, we must master one model or pattern. After that we can discuss variants in relation to our basic model, similar to the way we used one basic element and tied our analysis of compositions to that.

A *progression* is a set of occurrences which happens more than once. It should not be confused with progressing from one place to another, although that is a meaning of the word also. In music, progression usually refers to a set of chord changes which occurs over and over, serving as a basis for verses of a song or for improvisation.

The basic blues progression normally consists of twelve measures, each of which has four pulsations. To produce a measure we simply clap our hands four times, keeping the beats even. We can use the second hand on a clock, if we wish, to keep the time even. Next, we sing some note at the same time that we clap our hands, for instance, C, C, C, C or 1, 1, 1, 1. We have produced one measure with four notes. Next, we might want to produce two or four measures; usually a musical phrase will have four measures.

The blues progression consists of twelve measures of four beats each, which follows a certain pattern of scale notes. If each measure has four beats, one will have forty-eight beats, or pulses, in one progression of the blues changes. Using both letters and numbers, we can represent the blues progression as follows:

CCCC/CCCC/CCCC/CCCC/FFFF/FFFF/CCCC/CCCC/GGGG/FFFF/CCCC/CCCC//

or

1111/1111/1111/1111/4444/4444/1111/1111/5555/4444/1111/1111//

It could also be written this way, so that only the beginning beat of each four-beat measure shows the scale degree of the progression:

C///C///C///C///F///F///C///C///G///F///C///C///

or

1///1///1///1///4///4///1///1///5///4///1///1///

Development

The term *blues* is used in a variety of ways to describe very different phenomena. It can be used to describe a feeling of sadness or frustration. Certainly many of the early work songs illustrated such feelings and also some of the note patterns, that is, blueslike melodies. However, this is not the same as the blues progression just defined.

The blues can also describe a feeling in a song, or it may be part of the title, when in fact the song does not follow a blues progression. This of course confuses the issue still further, but for our purposes we will talk of blues songs which follow the basic twelve-measure progression given previously.

The history of the blues is significant, especially as we slowly work our way toward rock and roll. Early blues was rural blues, in the sense that it was performed by rural musicians in rural settings, usually as a solo (accompanied on guitar). It quite often followed patterns which were marginally like the blues progression presented in this book. Early blues forms had eight-measure lengths, ten-measure lengths, twelve, thirteen, fourteen, sixteen, twenty-four, and other odd lengths. Some were influenced by European dance forms, and others were simply produced spontaneously. The only overriding consistency was that they began as simple songs and then were improvised, both in lyrics and accompaniment, to fill out the remainder of the song. Improvisation is probably the most important trait of the blues.

Primitive blues was the primary form throughout the nineteenth century. Classic blues (as defined by LeRoi Jones in *Urban Blues*), the form which followed primitive blues, was the acculturated blues form. It was still not urban blues in the commercial sense, but it did begin to solidify the style and move toward a standard blues form.

By the beginning of the twentieth century, there were significant blues singers and instrumentalists who were influential in both the blues and most other forms available: Bill Broonzy, Leadbelly, Lightnin' Hopkins, Ma Rainey, Ethel Waters, Bessie Smith. Some later musicians in this same development are T-Bone Walker, Billie Holiday, Ella Fitzgerald, Muddy Waters, and B. B. King. Interestingly, some of these singers continued to employ eight-bar blues forms as well as the more standard twelve-measure phrase. The point is that each of these musicians did things which influenced other blues singers and eventually rock and roll. Even when they used progressions that did not follow the twelve-bar pattern, they used one to five changes and blues melodies.

Rural to Urban — The 1930s

In the 1930s, the blues took on a different character because of basic changes in society. Instead of being performed mainly for rural audiences or an imitation of rural audiences (Dixieland blues), the blues had become a vehicle for city blacks. In the 1930s, a counterculture to the white big-band era continued the popularity of the blues, but this time in a different setting.

Many black musicians developed big bands analogous to the white ones, and they were eventually quite competitive with their white counterparts. However, the blues singer continued to have great importance in an all-black circuit, which eventually fostered *rhythm and blues*.

The history of rhythm and blues is told in Arnold Shaw's *Honkers and*

B.B. King *(Used by permission of Fred Reif, Black Kettle Records, Saginaw, Michigan)*

Shouters: The Golden Years of Rhythm and Blues, and he very acutely points out between the lines that rhythm and blues did not just start in the 1940s and end with rock and roll. It has a history intertwined with the history of rural blues, assisted greatly by the boogie-woogie renaissance of the late 1930s and firmly established by singers like Robert Johnson and Joe Turner.

The style of these two musicians in particular illustrates the change brought about in the 1930s: The blues became stronger, angrier, and more like what is found in early rock and roll. Rhythm and blues is simply the addition of strong rhythm to the blues. It usually has elements of shouting, a characteristic which will later become a significant part of rock and roll.

Rhythm and blues probably was born the first time the blues was sung with accompaniment; some might say that black spirituals of the nineteenth century were incipient rhythm and blues. In any event, the history of the blues becomes the history of rhythm and blues in the 1930s, and it is precisely then that rural blues as such becomes more urbanized.

The difference between rural and urban blues is primarily one of culture. The urban dweller's problems differ from those of the rural dweller; he or she develops different artistic communications. Turner's blues form was called the *jump blues*, in that it was filled with terms like "rock'em," "shake it," and other utterances which will become part of the rock vocabulary. Jump blues was undoubtedly the beginning of rhythm and blues, if it did not occur earlier; and jump blues was the beginning of rock and roll as well.

RACE RECORDS

The final stages in the prehistory of rock and roll are found in the last part of the 1930s (the boogie-woogie craze) and in the 1940s. It is certain that a major reason for the emergence of rock and roll in the 1950s was the creditable market built up for race records (as recordings for the black community were called) in the 1940s. Significantly, although it may seem inconsistent, this era was blessed by the start of the removal of the color line between musicians.

Notable white musicians like Artie Shaw and Benny Goodman helped to remove the stigma about black and white musicians performing together — Billie Holiday with Artie Shaw and Teddy Wilson and Lionel Hampton with Benny Goodman. Although there continued to be distinctively black organizations — Basie, Ellington, and eventually Louis Jordan (the king of the black performers) — there also was relatively free interchange of ideas, and certain black styles began to slip into white organizations, if only by way of theft.

Race records, indies, or sepias (whatever they were called) were primarily rhythm and blues recordings aimed at black audiences. As black financial status began to build up in the war years (even more so after the war), there began to be a market for race records. Rhythm and blues was a staple of these small record companies, and there was a sizable if not millionaire status market for the recordings. Many of the rhythm and blues artists who eventually became significant in the 1950s (although perhaps not rich) paid their dues in the 1940s by making recordings for these small companies.

At first, the most interesting kind of recording was essentially boogie-woogie. By the mid-1940s, the form became an imitation of the white crooning tradition (the main leader at that time was Frank Sinatra), in which Nat King Cole was probably the most popular ("Mona Lisa," from 1949). All these recordings were sophisticated city songs designed for an urban audience. The significance of rhythm and blues, both as a continuing tradition and as a commercial art form, must be understood as the beginning of rock and roll. Although rhythm and blues is not rock and roll, the latter would not have existed without the former.

COUNTRY BLUES

Too little is made of the influence of country music on rock and roll, probably because of an unwillingness on the part of "hip" writers to accept the significance of white influence on early rock musicians. Much is made of the black singing style of Bill Haley and more particularly Elvis Presley, and we will certainly give due credit to their predecessors and to Haley's and Presley's black influencers. However, we must recognize that each was also influenced by country, or country and western, music.

Country music has two distinct styles — one is Southern and the other is Southwestern. The Southern style is the rural blues of the white culture of the rural South. It is characterized by simple folk songs dealing with everyday feelings, accompanied by simple rhythmic and melodic instruments. It is devoid of unusual syncopation. The Southwestern style developed slightly later (post 1930s) and is steeped in northern Mexican and cowboy life. It uses slightly more interesting melodic figures and more intense rhythm (although it is still rather simple). This form is sometimes called *Western swing* and tends to be somewhat instrumental in style when it is not singing about little dogies and/or horses.

The Southern style of country music was most influential in shaping early rock, in combination with black influences already discussed. The basis of this music is the isolation felt by poor whites in the South, and it shares some of the desolation of early black music. Although very much watered down in comparison to the earthiness of rural blues, it has some of the same singing techniques, in particular, sliding and flatted notes. Many Southern country tunes are based on blues progressions, although the words are clearly oriented toward white problems, in some ways similar to black problems. Whether these two styles (black rural blues and Southern country blues) have influenced each other is probably debatable, but they have both influenced early rock. Clearly, the term *rockabilly* (which many people use to refer to early rock and roll) comes from putting together rock and roll and hillbilly.

SUMMARY

1. All the following movements were significant in providing material for the beginning of rock and roll:

    black work songs

    spirituals

    cakewalk

    ragtime

Dixieland

stride

boogie-woogie

primitive blues

classic blues

jump blues

rhythm and blues

urban blues

country

2. Black singing style was most influential in the early history of rock and roll.
3. Most early rockers were rhythm and blues musicians and/or country musicians who were influenced by rhythm and blues.
4. Rock and roll can be defined as a song with a specific instrumentation and beat.

We see rock and roll as starting sometime in the nineteenth century and as developing at the same time as jazz. Therefore, the history of jazz is also the history of rock and roll. The blues, developing as a form of jazz and as an art in its own right, combined with jazz in the 1940s to provide the artistic material from which rock and roll came.

The marketability of race records in the 1940s provided the financial incentive necessary to induce musicians to develop a particular form that was a successful hybrid between white and black styles. Black musicians were the first rock and roll musicians, although it took white musicians to legitimize the form and to make it financially lucrative.

Once the form was solidified, it was possible to have free interchange between whites and black musicians; the development of free acculturation on the part of Afro-Americans became a reality, at least in the music business. *Rock and Roll then became the art form of racial interaction*, analogous to what happened in jazz (but interestingly enough, not until the same time). Therefore, to date precisely when rock and roll began is impossible, if we are to be consistent with these conjectures.

CHAPTER TWO

Early Rock–
Pre-Bill Haley

TYPES OF SONGS

Shouting

Many of the early rock tunes were rhythm and blues or jump blues. They used the blues progression, and the tempos were relatively fast. The lyrics were virtually shouted over the band background. This style of singing was made famous by the two musicians covered in Chapters Three and Four — Bill Haley and Elvis Presley — but it was earlier musicians who perfected it. Joe Turner, Leadbelly, Johnnie Ray, Fats Domino, Ivory Joe Hunter, Little Richard, and others performed in the shouting style, which was directly derived from rhythm and blues. This was the predominant style of early rock and the foundation for the careers of the famous rock musicians.

Many of these fast rhythm and blues tunes from the 1940s and early 1950s, some of which would be called rock and roll, used a backup band of five to six musicians — the Louis Jordan band, for example. On top of this constant playing, the singer would go through many verses of the song, each verse covering the span of one progression of the blues. This music was most definitely urban blues as opposed to the rural blues so significant to the early history of jazz. And it was quite different from the kind of pop music cultivated by the white population. It had little of the subdued emotion generated by the white population, and it most certainly retained the earthiness of black blues. It was at times sexually blatant, and it used the call-and-response pattern associated with Afro-American music.

Although the band played constantly, it also responded to the phrasing of the singer through background riffs, or simple melodies drawn from the lead melody. These background riffs served to answer the main singer and to reinforce the basic rhythms of the composition. As the singer ended a phrase, the instruments always filled in the empty spaces (those places where the singer was breathing). These riffs also served as the basic accompaniment figures when the singer was singing. This riff orientation was present in rhythm and blues, and it was also present in big-band style (although perhaps more so in black big bands).

One of the important traditions of the jump blues from the late 1930s and 1940s was improvisation, usually by the tenor saxophone. This style of playing, called *honking* or *wailing*, ultimately developed into a particular style of rock and roll saxophone, significant in the 1950s and then again in the 1970s. Improvisation by the saxophone player usually occurred in the center of the song to give relief from the constant singing. Ultimately it became a stylized function of a fast rock song. Although there are many tenor saxophonists noted for this style, we should certainly listen to Rudi Pompanelli, the saxophonist with the Comets; King Curtis, who played with Lionel Hampton and backed up the Coasters, Aretha Franklin, and others (he also recorded "Soul Twist" in 1962); and musicians more known for their contributions to jazz, like Sonny Rollins and John Coltrane. With the exception of Rollins, most of these tenor saxophonists were large men who projected strength through their instruments. This strong way of playing did emancipate the tenor saxophone from its role as the sweet instrument (the way it was played in the big bands). In fairness, Charlie Parker had quite a bit to do with emancipating the saxophone, but we should also give credit to the honking style of rhythm and blues.

Ballads

Ballad singing was also important in early rock and roll, although our theory is that ballads were seldom considered to be a part of the form, a distinction which was held for the shouting kind of rhythm and blues tune. Ballads were the real stock and trade of pop music, and whether the ballad was essentially a big-band tune, from the rhythm and blues tradition, or from country and western, it had a better chance for "crossover" popularity than the shouting tune did. For this reason, many musicians performed ballads, for both contrast and the real possibility of reaching larger audiences.

Although the history of ballad singing can be traced very far back in European music, the most significant starting point for a pop ballad is the crooning tradition in the United States. The first real pop culture crooner was probably Rudy Vallee in the 1920s and 1930s. The man who made "I'm Just a Vagabond Lover" famous sang through a megaphone (prior to amplification) and was essentially a big-band vocalist. But the significant point is that he held captive those people who heard him, and he had a profound emotional effect, especially on women. Vallee was a sex object before people used that term. Although he never directly influenced rock and roll, nor for that matter even liked it, he was influential in that he became a model for other crooners, singers with charisma.

Frank Sinatra was the crooner of the 1940s, and without a doubt he was the most important crooner of all time. He was the darling of a large majority of the women in America, and interestingly enough, he still is. Although primarily a big-band vocalist, Sinatra was the most copied crooner of that era, and many black musicians of the late 1940s and early 1950s acknowledge indebtedness to his style. Some might argue that Bing Crosby, Dean Martin, and others should be included here, but the point is that Frank Sinatra was important because of what he represented, his longevity in that image, and the influence he had on rock musicians. There were some black crooners of the late 1940s, like Cecil Gant, who clearly patterned themselves after Sinatra; they were called sepia Sinatras or black Sinatras. Nat King Cole is another good example.

Although the first vocal style of rock and roll — shouting — was based on the blues, the ballad was almost by definition never a blues song. We cannot give a model progression for a ballad because each one is different. The harmonic progressions were simple (although by the 1960s they would become more complex), and they were vocal in emphasis. Background singers were used either to sing in harmony with the main singer — as responding units using nonsense syllables — or to sing the melody with the lead singer. The ballad was not part of the mainstream of rock and roll until the mid-1950s, enjoying its greatest success between 1956 and 1958; it was considered to be just pop music before its inclusion in rock and roll. However, to discount its importance to the ultimate popularity of rock and roll would be like taking the heart out of a living human.

Novelties

The third kind of rock and roll song is a novelty tune, that is, a song with some gimmick which makes it catchy. Novelty tunes have always been important to a popular tradition, for example, the cakewalk or tunes like "Pennsylvania 6-5000" or "Chattanooga Choo-Choo," both by Glenn Miller. Although they are often short lived, some of them last a long time, if for no other reason than nostalgia.

Novelty songs have been important in the prehistory of rock and in the mainstream of rock as well (most notably in the 1950s style). Boogie-woogie songs were significant in the 1930s and 1940s, by both black musicians and white big bands. One of the first real big rhythm and blues tunes as a novelty was Stick McGhee's "Drinkin' Wine Spo-Dee-O-Dee" from 1949. Other examples are "Splish, Splash," all the twist tunes, and the monster songs like "One-Eyed, One-Horned, Flying Purple People Eater." "My Baby Loves the Western Movies" was an interesting example of crossover novelty (from country and western), although its commercial success certainly belies any musical taste.

STYLES OF SONGS

Rhythms

The rhythms of these kinds of songs can be quite easily classified by type. The shouting style usually uses rhythm and blues rhythms, which are consistent with the fast tempo of the songs. The rhythms are usually riff-oriented and are quite often derived from the long-short rhythm of boogie-woogie, with an underlying set of accents on beats two and four. This characteristic drum beat of 1950s rock in the fast tradition began to emerge in the late 1940s. The beat pattern eventually became standard for rock drummers in fast style, but with one change: Beat two was further subdivided into two equal half beats.

Beat one	nonaccented	O
Beat two	both halves accented	XX
Beat three	nonaccented	O
Beat four	accented	X

The rhythm of ballads is usually more oriented toward simple straight accompaniment, and there is seldom anything tricky or distinctive. Up until the mid-1950s, most ballad accompaniment was simply continuous and very light in texture. By the mid-1950s, one of the rhythmic styles for background ballad accompaniment (played by both the piano and the drums) was a subdivision of the four main beats into three sections each, which gave the measure a feel of having twelve beats, with emphasis on one, four, seven, and ten. We will see examples of this type of tune during the discussion of 1950s rock ballads.

The rhythm of novelty tunes is probably the most diversified and is frankly the most interesting in the 1950s style. Musicians used standard swing rhythm for novelty tunes in the late 1940s; this rhythm was derived directly from big-band drumming. By the mid-1950s, novelty tunes used many different rhythms, even within one song. Rhythm was also used for special effects, like banging on the drum to indicate knocking on the door. Novelty tunes depended on a large number of tricks to fill out the song and to provide as many catchy ideas as possible. Certain novelty effects in the use of the bass voice (for instance, by the Coasters) took on rhythmic significance.

Progressions

The shouting style basically uses the blues progression, although there are occasionally shortened versions of it or a gospel structure (see Ray Charles). The progressions are repeated many times, and the harmonies are not too hard to follow, even for an untrained ear. Most of the harmonies of fast songs have to be simple because they go by so quickly. In fact, fast songs are the one place where progressions are not extremely complicated, even as rock and roll evolves over time. There simply is not time to get very fancy, so the progressions are kept simple and the words and/or the texture is emphasized.

The ballad style has many different harmonic progressions, some simple and some more complex. Interesting harmony is sometimes used to emphasize particularly emotional parts of the lyric, but more often than not, the progression is simply a foundation for the all-important lyric. In ballads, there is a tendency to have one main melody for the verses, with a refrain or bridge section to provide contrast. Although clearly it would be nice if we could follow all the progressions in music, knowing each one of the chords in each ballad is not too terribly important in estimating the significance of the form. The importance of the ballad is in its emotionality, its impact, and its influence on the public, which is normally not harmonic.

Novelty tunes use simple progressions, and about half the time they are blues or modified blues. The other 50 percent of the time, they are folk song progressions. Again, the harmonies are occasionally used to emphasize novel aspects, but more often than not, these novel aspects can be explained in terms of the words or special effects, without resorting to harmonic analysis.

Backgrounds

The background figures (both vocal and instrumental) can be best categorized after listening to some examples of these different types of music. Although many of the background figures by singers are sung with nonsense syllables, they usually fit the context of the song. Background figures by instrumentalists are normally riff-oriented, taken from the main vocal. In fast songs, these riffs become the motivating force for the entire composition and often become the entire piece toward the end (see Ray Charles, "What'd I Say?"). Background figures are based on rhythm and blues in shouting songs and in some novelty tunes. Ballads use lush, smooth background figures, and novelty tunes use whatever works. Generalization past this point is difficult and should be made on a song-by-song basis.

CAPSULE VIEW OF THE 1950s

It is important to realize that the 1950s were to most Americans a time of great security. After World War II, the people prospered in ways they had never known before. Our involvement in the Korean War was thought to be successful from the point of view of national image. We saw ourselves as *the* world power, who had led the fight for democracy. When Dwight D. Eisenhower was elected president, we entered a period in American history where everything was all right, everyone was getting richer, and tomorrow would always be better than today.

During this era, there was a strong feeling of patriotism. Of course, this was a carry-over from the end of World War II, but we retained throughout the 1950s the feeling that ours was the best country in the world. We derived a certain sense of security in having Eisenhower as our leader and national symbol, in some sense the grandfather that we all desired. He was a great military leader; he represented anticommunism; and he would be able to provide good government for the people. Richard Nixon was appreciated for his involvement with Joe McCarthy against communism, most particularly in the House Un-American Activities Committee (HUAC). Our control over Nikita Khrushchev and the subsequent softening of the post-Stalin era made us feel that we were truly in power. In short, these were prosperous times, with a baby boom and more house ownership than ever before.

The economic solvency of many Americans was especially gratifying, and the postwar inflationary period which was predicted did not take place in the 1950s (we would have to wait for that). Although middle-class America felt prosperous, there were some elements of American society which seemed ripe for change, if not revolution. Some of these depressed groups were youths, blacks, and the lower class.

Senator Joseph McCarthy *(Used by permission of Folkway Records)*

The history of the black movement in the United States is significant throughout our discussions, but the most jarring changes were to take place during the 1950s. In 1957, the famous Selma bus incident occurred. By the 1960s, civil rights legislation would be taken seriously and finally enacted during Lyndon Johnson's administration. However, the seeds of discontent were sown in the late 1940s and the 1950s. Blacks had fought on the side of America during the wars. When they returned to the United States, they discovered quickly that they had been important during the national crisis but that their position had not changed in peacetime. Afro-Americans demanded a place in American society. They would not be going back to Africa, even though there were some movements later which would suggest that this plan still had supporters.

The promise of economic success led many blacks to assert their power in the 1950s, and at least some of this drive came from the fact that white society became rich by imitating blacks. Possibly the best example was rhythm and blues and ultimately rock and roll.

The young population in the 1950s is also relevant. With the growing affluence of young people as an off-shoot of parental affluence, there was a real market for their interests. Although it can be clearly shown that they were just as conservative as their parents in the early 1950s, this would be the first time that they had the free time (represented by peacetime and financial solvency) necessary to pursue their own interests. The change in attitudes about communism and war would come somewhat later, but youths' rebellion in terms of expressing their own values started early in the 1950s.

Lower-class Americans followed a similar pattern in that they wanted some of the affluence themselves. The labor union movement became strong in the 1950s, even during a Republican administration. This constant push on the part of the have-nots to become the haves was a source of rebellion; it could not be stopped once it started.

Therefore, the economic prosperity of the 1950s, the feelings of security, and the resulting attitudes of not worrying about tomorrow provided the opportunity for the lower class to begin asserting itself. Some called this the Marxist revolution in America; we would term it rational behavior.

MARKETING

Because of the cultural situation, rock and roll became a focal point for rebellion, and it must be understood in that context. In some senses it still is a focal point, although it has reached mass-communication levels in its present state. In the early 1950s, a Midwestern disc jockey named Alan Freed supposedly coined the term *rock and roll* as a replacement for *rhythm and blues*. He did so to make rhythm and blues more acceptable for broadcasting, especially as he had started running rhythm and blues shows at the Cleveland Arena. Rock and roll (at least its origins) most certainly was a conscious attempt to capitalize on the true marketability of music as a symbol for particular groups in society.

White youngsters had already developed a taste for black rhythm and blues, and the rock and roll revolution was certainly the result of a conscious desire to broaden that range of listeners. As a marketing technique, the invention of the term was very important. It separated the music from the racial connotations of rhythm and blues; it was something new; and it could be promoted as the music of youth. It is not clear whether it was an exploitation or simply a fad. The point is that it worked.

From 1947, when the Ravens sang "Ol' Man River," there was an available formula for slow ballads (see Chapter Five). There were more "bird" groups than you could possibly feed at the record store, and they basically followed one pattern of performance. The shouting style was also firmly established, and it had many talented practitioners. When rock and roll, as a legitimizing term, was invented, there was a vast amount of music which would ultimately be called by that name.

Early marketing techniques were primitive in comparison to later models (Elvis Presley and the Beatles, for example), but marketing was precisely what made this splinter movement into a multimillion dollar business. The stories of individual record companies, radio stations, and significant entrepreneurs of rock and roll provide information about individual progress (see the bibliography).

Of course, rock and roll was not immediately popular nor acceptable to the entire population of the United States. There were many people for whom it was a profoundly uninteresting phenomenon, a Communist plot, or just completely decadent.

The rock performer was seen as an image of pain, frustration, and rebellion. He or she was also admired and regarded as an interpreter of the dreams and desires of the population to which rock spoke. The reactions by those who were not part of that image were understandable, if perhaps overstated. As indicated earlier, there are still people today who view rock as nonmusic, with little redeeming value, or as just plain junk.

Our basic position is that rock and roll was formally named in the early 1950s, and that conscious techniques were used for these early songs. The elements of rock and roll were firmly established by 1951, and the performances of songs in this category provided the models for success. However, it took some force or charismatic character to serve as a focal point for the art form.

CHAPTER THREE

Bill Haley and the Comets

BIOGRAPHY

Bill Haley was born in Detroit in 1927. In the early 1940s (as a young teenager) he began playing country and western music; he was a relatively good guitar player. He toured with his band for six or seven years and then gave up music for a while, taking jobs with radio stations. At the end of the 1940s, he began shaping his band, the Comets, in a new style, which was a mixture of pop, country and western, and rhythm and blues.

Haley's career represents precisely what was discussed in the last chapter. He put together various forms of music that were popular for different segments of the society in the late 1940s. When he began to emphasize rhythm and blues elements in his music, he quite naturally retained some of his country and western roots, which is why much of his music was also called rockabilly.

In the process of making the transition to a white version of rhythm and blues, which culminated in 1951, he listened carefully to its popularizers in the 1940s, in particular, Louis Jordan. Haley copied the beat pattern of the jump blues and some of the performing antics of Jordan, who was really a consummate performer. When Haley finally renamed his group Bill Haley and the Comets, he had a clear view of what he wanted to do with his music and how he wanted it performed.

Haley's major contribution to the development of this form was probably in what he did to the lyrics of rhythm and blues tunes. He took the sexually obvious lyrics and changed them so that they were not quite so obvious. He really did not take the meat out of the lyrics; he just covered it with a disguise. In essence, he made the lyrics of rhythm and blues relatively acceptable to white audiences.

He also worked out elaborate stage routines, many of which were quite acrobatic. Although he himself did not move much, his musicians were known for assuming incredible poses when they were playing; for instance, the saxophone player would lean back and play with his instrument almost parallel to the floor. These stage techniques were already well known to black performers, but white performers were not used to this kind of motion. It did not go over well with people who were accustomed to the relatively staid performances of big-band musicians or groups like the Mills Brothers or the Andrews Sisters, but it went over very well with young audiences.

By 1951, Haley was ready to go out on the road again with his new group; they had a new style and a completely worked-out routine for performing it, neither of which was radically changed in later performances. It is important to realize that Haley was one of the few significant musicians in the history of rock who really did not change over the years. Virtually everyone else grew up with the times, including Elvis Presley, but Haley performed the same way in the 1970s that he did in the mid-1950s.

Haley's significance in rock was that he did it first in the complete sense of the word. He was not original, although he felt that he had invented rock and roll. He simply put together available elements at the right time and had the good sense to get them before the public. As a white representative of what black musicians had been doing for some time (and in many ways better than he ever did it), he was the catalyst necessary for rock and roll's success.

In 1951, he did quite well with a tune called "Rock the Joint." In 1952, he made "Crazy Man, Crazy," and in 1954 he made a cover of Ivory Joe Hunter's "Shake, Rattle and Roll." Also in 1954 he made "Rock Around the Clock." In

Bill Haley and the Comets *(United Press International Photo)*

1955, the film *Blackboard Jungle* came out and was aimed at a young audience. Its story of teenage decadence and alienation was backed up by soundtrack music by Bill Haley, including "Rock Around the Clock." This film really catapulted him into the limelight. In 1956, he made a film called *Rock Around the Clock*, which was an international success. After that he made another film entitled "Don't Knock the Rock," in which he was overshadowed by another performer. Little Richard seemed to be a better rocker than Haley, which put a dent in Haley's significance. However, Haley continued to make popular recordings, for instance, "See You Later, Alligator," "Corinne, Corinna," and "Green Door."

Haley was quite popular in England, where he toured in 1957. As his popularity was beginning to wane at home (in competition with Elvis Presley), England was still virgin ground. The people loved him there in 1957 and again in 1964. Although the Beatles and the Rolling Stones have not admitted to being influenced by Haley, they certainly must have been. His particular blend of musical styles was precisely what English rockers would do in developing their own unique style.

From the late 1950s on, Haley was a relatively minor figure on the rock scene, although he always evoked feelings of nostalgia and importance as the first big name. After all, he was not a terribly good musician to begin with, but he did perfect a model for rock and roll. Other musicians would do it much better, but Haley was the first white man to do it at all. He continued to put out single records and an occasional album. He played concerts; his fan club was alive and strong; and whenever there was a rock and roll extravaganza, he would usually be included. His performances were very consistent, but as other people surpassed him, he seemed to be poor in comparison. When he died in 1981, the obituaries were small; however, they all included the fact that he started the whole thing called rock and roll. As we have seen, this may not have been true, but he was the first to codify it and to be successful at it.

MUSICAL STYLE

The musical style of Bill Haley and the Comets fits the model definition of rock and roll, and in the 1950s it was a revolutionary concept. What Haley did was to put together a white rhythm and blues band; somehow he managed to use just the right elements in order to be successful as a white imitator of black music. It is highly questionable whether he would have been so successful had he only imitated, without changing, the black style.

Haley explained on the album *Bill Haley Scrapbook* (Kama Sutra 2014) that his band was working as a country and western band in the 1950-1951 era and that it was expected to perform country and western music. However, it would occasionally include a rhythm and blues tune with country instrumental arrangements. A close examination of that album, and in particular the song "Rock This Joint," will certainly illustrate this point. Although Haley would evolve a different conception of his music, he was basically a rock musician with a country background.

This particular song is a rather straightforward blues tune, with many repetitions of the blues progression. It is fast and clearly in the shouting tradition of rhythm and blues. In a short section (the first four measures) of singing at the beginning of his progression, Haley sings by himself with stop-time chords by the band. That is, he sings a little bit, and then there is a chord or two by all the musicians. After this short section, the band comes in and plays continuous background while he finishes the blues progression. The first part is from rhythm and blues and is the call-and-response pattern derived from African tribal music. The second part is straight country and western in back of a blues lyric.

With the exception of one rhythmic figure which will be mentioned later, everything in the background instrumental figures is country and western. The bass player usually plays on all four beats a walking bass pattern without noticeable accents. The drummer plays a straight swing-time drum pattern. The guitar solos are in country and western picking style, not at all like some of the great guitar rockers of the 1950s — Chuck Berry, for instance. The saxophone solo is melodic and sounds different from standard saxophone solos in the mid-1950s. In a live performance, they might look like rock musicians, but their playing style is not rock-oriented.

There is one rhythmic figure present in "Rock This Joint" which is significant. The following example has the rhythmic beats for two measures in numbers and small x's below the numbers which correspond to where the instruments play:

```
1 2 3 4 1 2 3 4
x   x   x x
```

For lack of a better explanation, this is a rhythmic riff, that is, a pattern which can be repeated over and over. This particular figure was used in a number of other traditions, for instance, in boogie-woogie, but it is also used throughout Haley's music and is central to the background accompaniment of "Rock This Joint." This riff happens to be a staple of 1950s rock and roll, and a number of musicians used it. It is appropriate that Haley used it in 1951.

The musical style of Bill Haley can be stated as follows:

1. rhythm and blues lyrics (watered down)
2. basically country and western instrumental playing
3. a stage routine designed to entertain and captivate the audience.

POPULARITY

The issue of popularity is one we will have to tackle at some point. We have already stated that just because something is popular, we need not assume that it is therefore automatically nonartistic. The real question is why certain music succeeds and other music does not. The first matter is success based on style; the second is success based on nonmusical issues.

Bill Haley put together a model of performing, based on his experiences of what popular music was. He combined elements of rhythm and blues — which he believed to be significant as a form of communication — and country and western. He also clearly understood that audiences would respond to visual entertainment. In essence, he applied logic to the production of a model for communication.

If artistic accomplishment is measured by the appropriateness of the ability to communicate ideas, popularity can be one measure of the relationship between art and its audience. We contend that the model of performing which Haley created was an appropriate one for communication because it took into account the audience and its needs.

One reason Haley's music was popular was that it used styles which were proven communicators for certain classes and types of people. By putting together models from different styles of music, he created a larger audience, which would relate to the new style as a combination of other styles. In essence, the music itself could communicate artistically to a certain population because that population already understood the elements of the new style, if only parts of it.

However, the interesting thing is that even though there were good reasons for this style to be accepted, it was not without controversy. The reaction against rock and roll, and in particular Bill Haley, intensified the significance of this particular form for those people for whom it was designed. The story of rock and roll is often told by who is against it rather than for it.

Although Haley enjoyed mild success with even his early recordings, especially "Shake, Rattle and Roll," it was not until the movie *Blackboard Jungle* came out that his audience gathered in his favor. There were so many critical statements made about Haley and rock and roll in 1955 and 1956 that he became an overnight sensation. Although we believe that the music itself should have guaranteed its success, it was the reaction against it which insured its popularity.

In particular, Haley's stage antics were thought to be crude. The white establishment did not accept entertainers who moved around a lot, unless it was Spike Jones or something slapstick. Bill Haley moved his legs; Elvis Presley was to move more. Even though the lyrics were quite watered down from the original songs, they were still perceived as evil. Many people thought the music was simply bad, and therefore they condemned it on that basis. As the music was a protest movement of sorts, this kind of reaction helped its popularity immensely. If it irritated our parents, it had to be good.

We have to understand that because the 1950s were prosperous, young people had a tremendous amount of free time. The attitudes of the majority were not acceptable to younger people, and many of them rebelled against these attitudes, although they may not have realized they were doing so at the time. When the press began to take up the cause and labeled rock and roll as part of a Communist plot, youth rallied in reaction. Haley and Presley might have lived their lives out as minor pop singers had the establishment (and occasionally the police) not decided that such singers were bad for the youth of our nation.

Therefore, we propose that part of Haley's popularity came directly from his opponents. Middle-class America still yearned for the days of the big bands, which died more for financial reasons than anything else. This new kind of popular music did not fit their image of what music should be, and besides, it was "dirty." As every generation is probably destined to rebel against the previous one, the young people of the 1950s rallied in favor of rock and roll — partly because their parents hated it.

NOSTALGIA

It is appropriate to deal with nostalgia here because Haley's popularity arose directly from a group that wanted something of its own. This same group would eventually see Haley as a re-creation of its youth. Nostalgia is significant for every form of music once it exists longer than ten years. As previously stated, Haley did not change his style over time. Therefore, all he had after his burst into popularity was the nostalgia of that particular sound.

Psychologically, nostalgia comes from the desire to reestablish contact with the past, usually from our youth. We all have yearnings from time to time to live the way we once did. Rationally, we cannot succeed, but music is an obvious way to remind us of the past.

It is not uncommon for people running high school reunion parties to hire a band which plays in the style popular at the time of graduation. In the 1980s, reunion committees hire big bands or 1950s rock bands. The big-band revival, which started in the mid-1970s, is based on nostalgia, as is the popularity of Sha-Na-Na and other 1950s groups.

Nostalgia does not involve music just from the 1940s and 1950s. It is also present in devotees to the early Beach Boys, those who hoped for a reunion of the Beatles (sadly now impossible), and even those who want a return to the folk-rock of the early 1970s. Nostalgia will always be present, if for no other reason than the psychological.

As society becomes more and more complex (and some say more depressing), nostalgia for the past will continue to grow. The continued popularity of Bill Haley can certainly be explained in terms of this phenomena. Haley's fans (even more so after his death) will continue to like his music for the following reasons:

1. It is simple and can be understood on an emotional level.
2. It represents the 1950s in all of its optimism (even though it was a rebellion against some of its attitudes).
3. It contains elements of commonly understood communication.
4. It is not sad or depressing.

One of the most important things about 1950s music is that, in comparison to contemporary music, it is uncluttered with deep messages, and especially, sad messages. Communication in general in the 1950s was optimistic and not complicated, and rock and roll is a reflection of this style.

We must not make too little of the fact that 1950s music was happy music. Although people were singing about the human emotions of pain, anguish, and frustration, it was not the frustration found in the 1960s and 1970s. We still trusted people in the 1950s, even if we should not have.

Bill Haley, then, represents his era, the 1950s, and all the optimistic things about those times. By continuing his style into the 1970s, he allowed us to recapture some of those golden moments, when everyone was rich, happy, and optimistic about tomorrow. The nostalgic feeling created by Haley's music is a potent one, and is one of the reasons why he enjoyed continued success.

THE DEATH OF ROCK AND ROLL

This may seem to be a strange place to bring up the possible death of rock and roll, but it has been a continuing story since the 1950s. Many people felt during the last half of that decade that rock and roll was just another passing fad. At first, it was probably wishful thinking on the part of conservatives, who really never liked it in the first place. However, by the early 1960s, it was a real concern because of a momentary lull (before the Beatles) in the speed and quality of the music's evolution.

The argument was taken seriously by a number of conservative columnists and radio announcers; naturally Bill Haley was one of the first rock musicians to be interviewed. He frankly admitted over the years that he was never really sure how long rock would last; but by 1964 he was completely convinced that it would survive, if only because there were other musicians who would add things to the form, which would make it last. He cited the contributions of Elvis Presley and later of the Beatles; over the years he gracefully gave credit to many other performers. If Haley and the style of his music were the entire history of rock and roll, it probably would not have been as significant; Haley contributed part of the history, however, and it was up to others to originate other variations.

Rock and roll did not die in the 1950s, because it was a vibrant form and because its detractors motivated the fans to support it. Rock in later generations survived because it kept changing with the times. It continues to speak in the language of the present, and its definition keeps getting bigger, bringing in more and more varieties of music.

CHAPTER FOUR

Elvis Presley

1. "Heartbreak Hotel"
2. "I Was the One"
3. "I Want You, I Need You, I Love You"
4. "You Ain't Nothin' but a Hound Dog"
5. "Don't Be Cruel"
6. "Love Me Tender"
7. "Any Way You Want Me"
8. "Too Much"
9. "Playing for Keeps"
10. "All Shook Up"
11. "That's When Your Heartaches Begin"
12. "Loving You"
13. "Teddy Bear"
14. "Jailhouse Rock"
15. "Treat Me Nice"
16. "Don't"
17. "I Beg of You"
18. "Wear My Ring Around Your Neck"
19. "Hard-Headed Woman"
20. "I Got Stung"
21. "It's Now or Never"
22. "A Mess of Blues"
23. "Are You Lonesome Tonight"
24. "I Gotta Know"
25. "Can't Help Falling in Love"
26. "Rock-a-Hula Baby"
27. "Return to Sender"
28. "Where Do You Come From?"
29. "Anything That's Part of You"
30. "Good Luck Charm"
31. "She's Not You"
32. "Devil in Disguise"
33. "Bossa Nova Baby"
34. "A Big Hunk O'Love"
35. "Stuck on You"
36. "Little Sister"
37. "Surrender"
38. "Ain't That Loving You Baby"
39. "Viva Las Vegas"
40. "I Feel So Bad"
41. "Kissing Cousins"
42. "One Broken Heart for Sale"
43. "A Fool Such as I"
44. "Wooden Heart"
45. "Crying in the Chapel"

This list represents Elvis Presley's gold records, awarded for selling one million copies each. During his career, he sold more than 400 million records. In this chapter we will discuss some of the reasons for his enormous success. It is our contention that Presley was a truly unique talent in the history of pop music and that he had some particular technical abilities which made him stand out from the rest of the performers of the 1950s.

Although Bill Haley was an important musician in the history of rock and roll, and he also stood as a national symbol for this particular movement, Presley had a quality which far surpassed Haley's, musically and personally. Presley had that important and rare personal quality called *charisma*, and his mere presence was awe-inspiring. We will walk a careful line between saying that the situation produced the possibility of his tremendous success or that he caused the situation and made the success. In any event, without Presley, rock and roll might not have lasted at all.

BIOGRAPHY

Elvis Aaron Presley was born on January 8, 1935; his twin brother, Jesse, did not survive. Vernon and Gladys Smith Presley were poor by anyone's standards, and when their son was born in Tupelo, Mississippi, they lived in a two-room house built by Vernon Presley. The family farmed the land on which the house stood; the land was barely capable of sustaining crops, but at times the Presleys had to live solely on what they could grow. During the war, Vernon worked in a war plant, which raised the standard of living of the Presley family to poor, just above indigent.

There were several important influences in Presley's early life in Tupelo, important in the sense that they can be traced throughout his career and in his music. He was raised in a strict manner, and his entire family was quite religious. He was raised as a Southern Baptist and this was important to him over the years. The second major influence was his mother, her love and her seeming ability to remain optimistic in the face of impending disaster. Certainly he was also affected by the fact of being poor.

Musically, Tupelo was a mixture of styles and ethnic backgrounds — English, Scotch, Irish, French, and African — coupled with Southern hillbilly and the nature of a small hick town. Tupelo was not a cultural mecca, but like many small towns it may have had more character than large ones; the musical character was significant in Elvis Presley's style.

The basic story of his life in Tupelo is one of poverty, although he was given the basic necessities of life — shoes, clothing, and food. His mother provided for her family as much as possible from their meager existence, but they did not have very much. They had to stuff cloth and other items in the holes in the walls during the winter to keep out the cold, and obviously both parents went without in order to provide for their child. Presley lived a simple life; he did not have many of the advantages of children in the 1950s and later. Of course, this particular kind of background would have an effect, and it should be clearly understood that his rise to fame and fortune was always bittersweet for the entire family. Unfortunately, Gladys Presley did not live long enough really to enjoy it.

When Presley was twelve years old, his father bought him a guitar for $12.95. Although this figure may seem minor to us, it was a major extravagance at that time, given their circumstances. Presley had already shown a great interest in music, and those around him knew that he had a good voice. However, there was never any intention that he would be a professional musician. He used the guitar as a diversion, listening to the radio and picking out tunes. Various sources are rather unclear about his real talent at this time, although it is known that he never had any formal musical training. Elvis Presley was a product of what he heard, his environment, and an awful lot of luck.

In 1948, the Presley family moved to Memphis, Tennessee, in quest of more opportunities for Vernon Presley. Biographers of Presley have tried to make something of this move in terms of his development as a musician, but the Presleys moved to better their lot in life and their son prospered for it.

Presley attended L. C. Hume High School and ultimately graduated in 1954. Other than having a strong interest in music, he was a mediocre student. Certain personality traits began to emerge at this time. L. C. Hume was predominantly black, and Presley was a big white boy. His only claim to fame

An original poster of Elvis Presley for a 1956 concert *(Poster owned by Bill Kehoe, Bay City, Michigan. Photo by Barry Rankin)*

in high school was his hair, which he spent hours on and which probably irritated his peers. He performed in a school talent show, and according to contemporary accounts, he became a minor hit because of his emotional style of performing. Also, he had an impact on the girls in the crowd, although certainly not at the level which would occur later.

It is truly amazing that facts about his early career are so clouded, especially because these events were happening in the 1950s, but this underscores the fact that Presley was not being schooled as a professional musician. He was just an average kid trying to get through high school. He competed in a singing contest at the Alabama-Mississippi fair at the suggestion of his high school principal, and he won with a favorite song of his mother's called "Old Shep." Sometime between 1953 and 1954 he made a demonstration record of "My Happiness" and "That's When Your Heartaches Begin." This record, made for his mother as a present, cost Presley four dollars. Although it normally would not have led to anything, in this case it did.

At some point in this book, we really should discuss the probability of achieving success as a professional musician, especially big success. The chances are one in a million. Like many heroes of success stories, Presley was at the right place at the right time. He did not have professional training, he had no contacts, and he received no assistance from important relatives or friends. No one should rationally assume that he or she will be successful as Presley was. Of course, that will not stop people from trying, but most people who try to follow in Presley's shoes will end up with sore feet.

Probably the most important person in the development of Presley as a marketable item was Sam Phillips, who just happened to be the sound engineer when Presley came in to cut his four-dollar demonstration record, or demo. Phillips was in the process of beginning a small record company, ultimately named Sun Records. Although most small record companies die shortly after birth, Sun Records went on to become one of the most significant small companies of the 1950s, launching the careers of Jerry Lee Lewis, Johnny Cash, and Elvis Presley, among others.

Of course, demos are one of the means by which an unknown performer can become recognized, and record companies have set up full-time business for creating these records. In the 1950s, small record companies would make demos for a small amount of money, and these short production items would help to cut the overhead costs of the company. The demos were basically designed for the performer only, and there was no promise of putting them out on the market. Today, demos can cost up to $10,000, although unfortunately the results are usually the same; the performer is left with a record and nothing else.

The record Presley made was not sold, but Phillips was impressed with the basic sound of his singing voice. Presley later said that this recording sounded like "somebody beatin' on a trash can lid," but something about his voice influenced Phillips, who told Presley that when his company got started he would contact him.

In the meantime, Presley had graduated from high school and had taken a job as a truck driver. He had worked as an usher at a movie theater, and the move to driving a truck was a natural one for him because he was interested in cars and mechanics. He made thirty-five dollars a week, and this was in 1954, although his financial picture would change quickly over the next two years. Phillips did contact Presley later in that year and Presley cut his first real record.

Phillips helped Presley form his first musical group, The Starlight Wranglers, which included Scotty Moore on piano and guitar and Bill Black on bass. Obviously, this was basically a country and western group in the southern tradition, and frankly it was not very successful. Both Moore and Black were significantly better musicians than Presley. However, Phillips kept them together for an eventual recording, and they spent quite a bit of time at the Sun studio.

Apparently without guidance, Presley sang a song called "That's Alright, Mama," originally done by Arthur ("Big Boy") Crudup, an important rhythm and blues singer. In the same session at the Sun studio, Presley suggested another tune called "Blue Moon of Kentucky," by Bill Monroe, a white singer who was known as the father of bluegrass. These two songs were put on a record, which sold over seven thousand copies locally. The sale was accomplished through the help of a local disc jockey, Dewey Phillips (no relationship to Sam). Although a minor success by national standards, this recording can be credited as Presley's real beginning.

A point which should be made here is that Presley had diverged from the original intention of the musical group formed to back him up. He was singing black blues in an unmistakably black style. He sounded like a black singer with a country and western instrumental style. Although his judgment of the record as being "trash can" music may have been accurate, it was the combination of his voice in a black style with southern instrumental accompaniment which would eventually become his personal mark of success.

At this time another disc jockey entered his life. Bob Neal took over as his manager and renamed the group the Blue Moon Boys, which was taken from "Blue Moon of Kentucky." Neal had many contacts in the area, and he began to book the group at dances and auditoriums. Neal and Presley began to create Presley's image, particularly his singing style and stage presence. Frankly, he was not terribly successful during that year, although he was beginning to earn as much as $200 a week. Although there were continuing difficulties over his black image, his obvious sexuality, and his nonconformity, Presley was becoming a sex symbol and not without true impact. Neal was careful as a manager, although not as successful as Presley's next manager would be. He built Presley's career slowly, and by the end of 1955 was grooming him as a national star. He arranged for an audition for the "Arthur Godfrey Show," which was unsuccessful.

During the summer of 1955, Neal began to feel pressure because of his commitment to Presley, and he contacted "Colonel" Tom Parker about taking over. Parker was a very successful manager of musicians, including Eddy Arnold and Hank Snow. Although Sam Phillips was most influential in the beginning of Presley's career, it was Parker who made him really big. Parker took over toward the end of 1955 and turned an emerging career into a monumental one.

Parker arranged for a release from Sun Records, selling Presley's contract to RCA Victor. He obtained an appearance for Presley on the "Jackie Gleason Show" with the Dorsey Brothers, the "Steve Allen Show," and eventually the "Ed Sullivan Show." Parker also pulled off one of the most significant marketing tricks in the history of rock and roll; he signed Presley for movies. Parker's concept was a package deal. Presley would do the movies and then they would release the songs from the movies, first as singles and then ultimately as albums.

When Presley released "Heartbreak Hotel" in January 1956, he quickly

Elvis Presley *(Courtesy of RCA Records)*

got his first gold record, and the television appearances, concerts, movies, and recordings became one gigantic package. Parker engineered the whole thing, and Presley became a multimillionaire as a result. The press certainly helped, especially the press which talked about Presley's sexuality, from both a negative and a positive view. The fact that Presley was condemned by many people probably did a great deal to enhance his "aura" and charisma.

In 1958, Presley was inducted into the army, and in a stroke of masterful image building, he accepted induction without complaint. Whether or not he actually was patriotic, this gesture endeared him to people who previously condemned him. In a sense, he legitimized himself in the eyes of his detractors, who still might not like his music but had to appreciate him as a symbol. After all, Presley was accepting his role as one of the people and also as a symbol for youth. It also took him off the market for a while, which actually insured his success after a two-year absence. Fortunately, Parker had plenty of Presley material to work with during this hiatus.

During basic training in the United States, Presley returned home to be with his mother, who had become sick. The illness was diagnosed as hepatitis, and there was every expectation that Gladys Presley would recover. However, she suffered a heart attack and died in July 1958. Presley was deeply affected, as his mother was probably the most important person in his life. During 1957 he had purchased a large mansion, Graceland, in Memphis, and the rest of his family returned there. Presley went to Germany for his military service, but there is no doubt that he was deeply troubled that his mother was not alive and enjoying Graceland, which certainly must have been purchased with her in mind.

While in Germany, Presley met Priscilla Beaulieu, who would become his wife in 1967. When he met her she was still a teenager, and Presley had her brought to the United States, where she lived with his parents and went to school. It seems that she led a very sheltered life and that Presley was grooming her as a wife and mother, almost maintaining her until she became of age. This is one of the hardest things to understand about Presley; however, he did love Priscilla and their child, Lisa Marie.

Returning from the service in 1960, Presley was immediately thrust back on the American scene in a movie called *GI Blues* with Juliet Prowse. His career was certainly significant in the 1960s, although it was mostly tied to movies, which became the focal point of the marketing package. At least until the Beatles became popular, Elvis was still the hottest property around. He began gradually to stop giving concerts and making appearances, reserving most of his time for Graceland (with his new family and a new stepmother), recordings, and movies.

For the rest of the 1960s, Presley was seldom seen in public and seldom performed for live audiences. From the late 1960s until his death in 1977, his performances were mainly in Las Vegas, where he continued to pack the house. The so-called declining years became filled with stories about his obsessions, weight, drugs, and battles with reality. He most certainly was a vibrant personality until the end; however, the naive simplicity of his early career was gone. He had become an extremely complex and rich middle-aged man.

We are tempted to say that Presley did not evolve with the times, but a careful listening to his recordings from the end of his career would suggest the opposite. Retained in his music were country and blues roots, but the instrumental backing was constantly updated. He used contemporary music where

Elvis *(Courtesy of RCA Records)*

Elvis *(Courtesy of RCA Records)*

it fit, and his performances made use of modern technology — additional musical resources and contemporary subjects. Although Presley was tied to his background, he changed as his background changed. His last performance in Las Vegas was exciting and filled with energy.

MUSICAL STYLE

The following comment by Carl Wilson of the Beach Boys says quite a bit about Presley's music:

> His music was the only thing exclusively ours. His wasn't my mom and dad's music. His voice was a total miracle, a true miracle in the music business.

This comment was made right after Presley died, but it sums up what could be said about his music from the start. All of the elements of his style added up to music which was for youth and exclusively for youth. It is important to realize that he was successful because he became identified with the needs of youth, regardless of what their parents thought.

Like Bill Haley, Presley combined elements of white and black culture, but his singing was primarily black in style. His first recording was of tunes by blues singers who had influenced him — one black and one white. Many of the elements of those early records could be analyzed in terms of the original sources. His vocal inflections, his choice of rhythmic accents, and the instrumental ensemble must be understood in relation to the particular combination of elements in his individual style.

In fact, many of his early problems in achieving success were tied to his musical style. He was a white country and western performer who sang rhythm and blues. Most disc jockeys would not play his records because they could not play blues tunes in a country and western format, or they could not play country and western tunes in a blues format. He was caught in the middle.

Lyrics

Most of Presley's tunes had watered-down black lyrics, at least at the beginning. Although some of the tunes were written by white lyricists, for instance "You Ain't Nothin' but a Hound Dog," the content and structure of the lyrics are very much like black rhythm and blues. At first Presley recorded two basic types of songs — shouters and ballads. The shouters used blues progressions (or modified blues progressions) with call-and-response technique. The ballads had slow rhythm and blues formats. Later, Presley's ballad style would be more influenced by white tradition, in particular, by hymns. He was a crooner in the black tradition who later expanded his vocabulary to include songs from a white tradition.

The lyrics were usually fairly simple, and they were consistently emotional. They expressed rural feelings, and until the 1960s, seldom were there expressions of the leisure-class rich — rock and roll parties and foreign places. Obviously, his movies had a great deal to do with lyric choices, but these were not natural choices for Elvis Presley. The lyrics followed very simple struc-

Elvis in concert, 1977 *(Photo by Barry Rankin)*

tures — the blues progression in short lyric patterns in the fast tunes, and simple song structure in the ballads. All Presley's songs were lyric-dominated, and his voice and the words were the most important qualities, even when he was using nonsense syllables or gutteral sounds as emotional expressions.

Vocal Tricks

Probably the most significant part of Presley's talent came from his voice. He had one of the most naturally gifted voices to come out of the history of rock. He did not have formal training at all, so his voice was developed through listening and imitating, but it must be understood that he had a natural ability to sing. His vocal range was quite large — from baritone to deep in the bass range — and he used the entire range to communicate effectively a large number of emotional feelings.

He made extensive use of *vibrato*, a wavering of the pitch designed to color the note or to make it sound fuller and more emotional. Unlike many musicians, he used vibrato with a great deal of sensitivity and variability, a most important quality in good music. When a particular passage called for a straight tone, he would do that. When it called for a heavy vibrato (very wide and punctuated), he could do that also. He had ultimate control of the vibrato, and he either naturally used it well or he learned to do so.

He also made extensive use of *vocal slides*, beginning a pitch and dropping it off at the end (or sliding up to a note), for example, in "Love Me Tender." As you might recall, vocal slides were a predominant feature of work songs and field hollers and early blues and gospels. The vocal slides were used in conjunction both with significant lyrics and with nonsense words. Some people have called these vocal slides sexual utterances.

Presley also made use of a technique employing a *glottal stop*. The glottis is a flap of skin which cuts off the breathing function, especially useful when drinking. It allows the singer to control how the musical note ends or begins. By cutting off the note in a certain way, he or she can produce a strong sound for emotional reasons or for accenting. Presley made extensive use of this technique for emotional or sexual purposes. In fact, some people have said that he could make women faint simply by moving the glottal flap.

Presley had a marvelous ability to move back and forth between full voice and soft voice. He used musical contrast to the utmost, which for strictly musical reasons is quite effective. However, he also used it for audience response. By softening his voice for certain passages he could create a personal effect, which made the women in the crowd feel that he was singing directly to them.

Another ability of Presley was the contrast between his straight singing voice and shouting. This is clearly a gospel technique and relates rather interestingly to the call-and-response technique discussed in earlier chapters. He could change in the middle of a song from one style to another, thereby enhancing communication with the audience. Fortunately, all these techniques worked on records as well.

These vocal tricks and others produced a total sound which was consistently interesting. Presley was a very involving performer, and even without his physical movement, he was captivating. Although this could be debated, his movies probably would not have been successful because of plot alone. They were clearly vehicles for Presley to show off his singing and his body.

Elvis *(Courtesy of RCA Records)*

Stage Presence

Normally when we discuss a particular singer we will include the background musicians and their impact on a performance; however, in Presley's case the background musicians probably did not have very much to do with the effect. The stage presence was the presence of Presley alone. He was called the "King" because he commanded everything all by himself. Bill Haley could not do that, but Presley was able to hold the audience's attention in a decisive way.

His stage movements were designed to fit what he did with his voice, and they must be understood in this connection, although they are significant as part of the package. These consisted of general body movement; the shape of his mouth; and movement of the head, hips, and arms. Each of these movements came naturally to Presley, although clearly he used them more and more as they worked.

At this point we should settle the issue of whether Presley meant to be nasty or not. We take the position that he was not being dirty or sexual but that these motions came to him naturally. Whether or not this premise is true, Presley's sexuality had a great deal to do with his enormous success. People *thought* he was sexual, and the ones who liked that sexuality appreciated him more for it; those who did not like it made him more popular through their negative comments.

Presley's movements, quite natural during fast tunes, almost cost him his career at first. People did not like those contortions in a white singer. But as he gained acceptance, the motions became part of his image. He just generally moved at the right times. When he wanted to make a point in a particular song, he stopped moving. That told the audience it was time to pay attention.

Presley had a natural sneer; that is, the right side of his mouth was quite often a little more open than the left. When he was singing a strong vocal line or when he was portraying a tough or a hurt image in a film, he naturally went into the Presley sneer. It was an effective and natural act, and it worked.

He was called "Elvis the Pelvis" because of the way he worked his hips. This movement, which was most certainly natural, conveyed an obvious sexuality (whether or not he meant it to), but it was also very rhythmic and accented the beat of the song. He seldom used the hip movement in slow songs because the songs did not need it. He did use hip movement or pelvic thrusting in slow songs to make a point, but again the key matter is that he used the movement to enhance the feeling of the song.

He also used his head, hands, and arms to emphasize particular aspects of a song, to reach out for the audience. His performances were very visual, but it was the combination of his movement with his singing that made them so captivating. He would at times project the image of a folk singer for songs like "Are You Lonesome Tonight?" or for religious songs. He was a master at using body motions to communicate, and he showed this mastery by occasionally using no motion at all.

Religiosity Versus Sexuality

It is tempting to treat Presley as if he were all body and no mind, but an objective view of his life would suggest that he was a fairly complex person. He came from a humble background, and at one time he was content to be a truck driver and part-time musician. He loved tinkering around with automobiles and he later showed that he had an obsession for material things. He obviously needed to be loved, handling some of his power and charisma rather poorly. However, he gave of himself to others, and in so doing, showed that he had real human concern. In fact, his financial advisors often feared that he would give away everything.

It is also easy to dismiss each of Presley's actions of charity, patriotism, and reverence as part of the big package designed to sell the star. However, a careful look at some of these will reveal that they usually happened when he was not being controlled by someone else. And even when they were advantageous to his career, this was an afterthought rather than premeditated. In short, Presley was honestly giving and patriotic and equally honest in his respect and love of God.

To trace his religious feeling, it is important to return to the First Assembly Church of God in Tupelo. Presley's mother had a great deal to do with his religious upbringing, regularly taking him, even as a baby, to church with her.

Although we can be skeptical about this story, it is reported that by the age of two he could carry a tune without being able to sing the words of the hymns. His mother supposedly had a good voice, and she certainly must have sung hymns around the house; Presley would not have sung these songs throughout his life had it not been for his mother. It is hard to presume that he did not believe in the messages of these songs, even if at times he may not have necessarily reflected on them.

But Presley was also sexual, both in action and in singing. Although his singing style would suggest a preoccupation with sex, some of his actions in the early years would argue against that view. In the early 1950s, he had a desire to be seen with women, his ultimate goal being to marry the right one. His relationship with Priscilla, at least until he married her, appears to have been relatively puritanical. He seems to have used sexuality as a cover story rather than as an end in itself.

Presley started out as a simple country boy, and during the rise to fame, he retained many of his country roots. He commented on being able to buy indoor plumbing and cars, in fact, just being able to buy anything at all. He was a classic example of the *nouveau riche*, newly acquired wealth. For a time, he retained all the old values. Even in the 1960s, he would often get underneath cars in order to tinker with them. We can see many of those country roots, in his singing and in his life, and remnants of them in his lifestyle, even when he went to excess.

Religiosity and sexuality, then, should be seen as two extensions of his personality and beliefs. They are not contrary attitudes. They express the same dichotomy as white country and western and black rhythm and blues. Elvis Presley put both pairs together — musical as well as philosophical.

Style Development

Style development is normally thought to be the province of "serious" artists. However, rock musicians go through stylistic changes just like other artists, and these should be taken seriously. It is precisely this kind of continued change which makes rock and roll vibrant.

Elvis Presley did not change as much over the years as did the Beatles or the Beach Boys (Chapters Seven and Eight), but he did go through some different periods: the first between 1952 and 1958; the second, 1960 and 1965; and the third, 1965 and 1977. Each period, or stage, could be defined in terms of stylistic traits, and there is variability among the stages.

Stage 1 (to 1958) can be characterized as the formative period, in which Presley combined the elements of his musical environment and came up with the basic package. He clearly combined black rhythm and blues with white country and western (Southern style), established his basic stage presence, and marketed himself as a singer and performer. In this style, he was a model of 1950s music and could be analyzed in terms of our definition of rock and roll. He was emotional and somewhat simplistic. Although the technical level of his performances was good, there was little sophistication in the background music or the recording techniques.

Stage 2 (1960 to 1965) is basically the movie period, in which his singing was the focal point for a somewhat larger audience. His singing remained basically the same, although the background became greater. The instrumental ensemble was enlarged (using studio musicians as a backup group), even though the ensemble shown on the screen was still a rock and roll band. However, the setting of the performance was extended to real life experiences, if we can call singing on a beach in Hawaii a real life experience. The stage had been extended to the world, and this must be seen as a definite change in style; he had become broader in scope.

Stage 3 (1965 to 1977) is usually overlooked in discussions of Presley because of the troubles he had during these times. However, this later part of his life contains some of the best examples of his use of advancing technology and a real updating of musical materials. Most of the songs were the same, and there was a great deal of nostalgia in his late performances. However, even when he sang an older song, he usually made a change in the musical background. Advanced technology was used to make the background sound bigger, similar to the way the Beatles used larger musical resources in their later albums.

A careful listening to his last album, *Elvis in Concert*, will illustrate the last point. He used a big band to back up these performances from a tour in June 1977. From the very beginning of the record, the presence of the large ensemble changed the basic sound of a Presley performance. That is, although his voice was still the most important thing, the addition of the big band changed the overall sound. The theme song was an up-tempo, simple riff composition that was really not rock and roll at all; it was show music. There was a brief performance of an arrangement of the *2001* theme, which went back into the riff to introduce Presley. It was a very effective stage device, but more significantly, the big band continued to be important in all the songs on the album. It provided a contrast with a rhythm ensemble, used for backing up Presley's singing; the band, and at times a backup vocal group, was used to fill in the empty spaces. Guitar solos were typically country and western in orientation.

The most interesting thing about these very late recordings is that even Presley changed. If we listen carefully to a song recorded in 1977 and then the same song recorded in the 1950s, we will notice some changes in vocal inflection and range (he seemed to be weak in the upper notes in 1977), but more important, there were at times differences in rhythmic feel. Whereas earlier tunes reflected country accenting, there was a definite funk or disco feel in his later ones. It is a subtle point but a very important one. Presley was influenced by other musicians and the prevailing way of making music. If you listen carefully, you can hear where those influences changed his style.

On a general level, the later music also had a kind of vibrancy, which some of his earlier material did not. The difference was made primarily by the addition of more musicians, better musicians (that is, studio players), and better technology. Even the microphones used in these later recordings were infinitely better than those from the 1950s (see Chapter Ten).

Impact

The most significant impact of Elvis Presley was his success. By being successful, he opened up markets for other musicians and served as a symbol for the development of marketing techniques, for technological advancement in electronic equipment, and for the significance of a charismatic character. We had heroes in the United States before, but the magnitude of Presley's stature was probably larger than any other performer. He was also important in that he combined white and black elements.

The marketing techniques used to accelerate Presley's impact were not new; they were based on previous models, which had been successful on a large scale. However, these marketing techniques had a multiplier effect because of the cash flow available in the 1950s. The significance of Colonel Parker is major: He was the guiding force behind the creation of an entertainment complex, first through performances, then television, and finally movies.

It is noteworthy that Parker used so many resources for creating this complex. He realized the potential of the new developing medium — television — and coupled Presley with Steve Allen, the Dorsey brothers (still popular from the big-band era), Ed Sullivan, Milton Berle, and others. During a time when the motion picture industry was being hurt by the intrusion of television, Parker created a package for Presley in the movies. His pictures made a lot of money for the movie industry and pointed the way toward the kind of movies that would draw people back to the theaters; ultimately the same pictures were sold back to the competition — television. The records, which came from the movies, and all the other paraphernalia — T-shirts, pictures, fan clubs — made each part of the package more lucrative. These models were copied in each successive generation and allowed the creation of new stars — the Beatles as an artistic example and the Monkees as a financial one.

It is interesting that the financial empire created around Presley ultimately returned completely to the family, the unit which was so important to him. Vernon Presley became the financial controller of the entire estate, and although he was educated only through the eighth grade, he seemed to do well. Elvis Presley trusted his father more than anyone else, and he gave him power of attorney over everything. It was a great credit to his father that he retained so much of the Presley wealth for his son. If we are to believe the stories, Elvis Presley might have given it all away if his father had not had some control. Of course, the tremendous wealth of this family required the services of financial advisors, which Vernon made use of when necessary.

HIS LEGACY

Elvis Presley influenced a tremendous number of rock musicians, some who had started before him and many who followed him. Bill Haley in later years indicated quite clearly how important Presley was and how much he had influenced the Comets and others. The Beatles acknowledged that Presley was very important to them. Mick Jagger, Pete Townshend, the Beach Boys, Fats Domino, Tom Jones — all of these major performers have acknowledged a debt to Presley. But whether or not performers recognize what he did, virtually every rock and roll musician uses a Presley technique at least every once in a while.

His singing style, his stage presence, and the techniques used to build his career were all influential. But the lasting legacy of Elvis Presley is his success. Had it not been for the strength of his personality, he might have been just another good singer with a unique performing style. However, he had that rare quality to generate power over people simply by the way they felt in his presence. That charismatic strength is something all rock and roll musicians either have or rebel against.

Presley must remain a central figure in rock and roll. For all the reasons stated in this chapter, if we had to choose one musician from the 1950s as the most important rock figure, we would have to choose Elvis Presley.

CHAPTER FIVE

Broadening of the Style

THE END OF THE FIRST ERA

This chapter discusses the late 1950s and the mature style of rock and roll. Some of the music mentioned will in fact be from the very early 1960s, as the beginning of the next era does not really start until the Beatles. As usual, in any transition period there are continuations of the basic style into the next era.

Rock and roll is the term we used to describe music from the 1950s; in later chapters we will begin to use the term *rock*, for reasons which will be discussed later. Rock and roll began to encompass more music in the late 1950s than it did within the early period. That is, although the style was still fairly homogeneous, late rock and roll included several types of music that would not have been considered rock and roll earlier. It is important to realize that rock and roll was really not legitimized until the late 1950s, and that it took the developments discussed in the first four chapters to create the basis for mass popularization. The distinction between pop and rock and roll was real until the late 1950s. By 1958 there was no real distinction. An examination of the songs at the top of the *Cashbox* and *Billboard* ratings will illustrate this point. Therefore, we will expand our categories of tunes to define five basic types rather than the three of Chapter Two.

This particular period at the end of the 1950s is sometimes called the "decadent" period in rock and roll because of its commercialization. There was clearly an attempt on the part of the artists to communicate on a broad spectrum, and it sometimes led to songs that had little vitality because they were further watered down from the original black or country roots. Although this description is fairly accurate, it should not be seen as a condemnation of this period. It should be viewed as a solidification of the style rather than a selling-out. It would take the Beatles to revitalize the progressiveness of rock and roll, but it should be remembered that the Beatles performed in the style described in this chapter until at least 1964.

Five Types

By the late 1950s, we can see five specific types of rock and roll: rhythm and blues, shouting, crooning, specialty songs, and novelty/monster songs. Of course, these are extensions of the three types discussed earlier.

There continued to be a vibrant group of performers in the rhythm and blues tradition. Many of them were considered to be simply rockers, but musicians like Chuck Berry and Fats Domino still remained in the rhythm and blues style. Although it may be hard to distinguish their music from 1950s rock and roll, it must be remembered that their rock and roll was rhythm-and-blues-oriented. Crossover (appealing to more than one audience) was essential to the success of a 1950s musician, even though he or she might retain the roots of one particular style. In fact, the concept of crossover is essential in explaining the phenomenal success of Bill Haley and Elvis Presley.

Rhythm and blues as a separate form began to fade in the late 1950s, and by 1963 it was removed from the *Billboard* ratings. However, there was a continuing interest in rhythm-and-blues-oriented tunes, although they were then called pop tunes. The Motown complex in Detroit, which began in the early 1960s, was aimed at the mainstream pop market, although clearly the emergence of soul did rely heavily on black listeners.

Chuck Berry *(Used by permission of Fred Reif, Black Kettle Records, Saginaw, Michigan)*

Shouters continued to perform during this period, although in some senses they were a continuation of the earlier style. One of the best shouters of the late 1950s was Little Richard, who really took over from where Bill Haley left off. Elvis Presley was an influence in the shouting style, and of course, this was one of his most effective techniques. This style did not change substantially in the late 1950s, but it did become more sophisticated and also more effective.

Crooning was probably the most important style of this period, and rock and roll ballads were extremely important in the rapid commercialization of the art form. By the late 1950s, rock and roll was the principal medium for youth dances, and ballads provided necessary relief from the style of dancing to fast songs. (We will discuss this topic at some length shortly.)

Specialty songs are those which are associated with some dance step or some special attitude. Although they could be labeled novelty tunes, they are usually somewhat broader in communication. Some of the most important dance steps (often fads) had songs written specifically for them, for example, the twist or the fly.

It would be easy to dismiss novelty songs as cheap commercialization were it not for the fact that they have remained popular over the years. Some of the best examples are "monster" songs and tunes by groups like the Chipmunks (David Seville). Although these songs are perhaps shorter lived than any of the other types, they are good examples of the commercialization of the form during this period. They usually have some rock and roll characteristics, but they are sold to the general public as either pop or rock and roll.

Free Acculturation

By the late 1950s there was free interchange among the various types of music and the market was not necessarily segregated. As long as songs fit into certain models, they were accepted with relative indifference to the racial origin of the musicians.

Later in this chapter, we will take the position that it was Ray Charles who finally legitimized this compromise position, but it should be understood that the market already freely accepted it. It had been established by Bill Haley and also by Elvis Presley. Rock and roll was a combination of black and white models; therefore, rock and roll became the focal point for what we refer to as free acculturation.

This is not to suggest that there did not continue to be music for black audiences and for middle-class white America. But anything designated or thought of as pop or rock and roll usually was accepted by both white and black audiences, that is, those black and white audiences who liked that kind of music.

Opportunities for black musicians were still fewer than for white ones, and there were white musicians who essentially made cover recordings (and we might add, made a lot of money) of songs originally sung by blacks. However, as both white and black musicians discovered the money potential in songs which were compromises, they began to overcome racial differences. Although we stated earlier that Elvis Presley was the most important musician of the 1950s, other significant musicians of that time were Chuck Berry, Little Richard, and Ray Charles — all three of them black.

Urban to Commercial

The first step in the path toward rock and roll was the change from rural to urban blues, which occurred before the name was formally coined. Urban music, of course, is city-oriented and carries with it a certain number of expectations. It must speak to the needs of city people rather than the farmer or craftsperson. However, being oriented toward city life does not mean being commercial and/or financially successful. All too often people assume that urban means commercial.

Urbanization led to the circumstances in which rock and roll could be marketed, and certainly most of the marketing techniques already discussed were centered in large cities. However, the commercialization of rock and roll transcended urban and rural distinctions once it got started. The marketing techniques were aimed at people in small towns as well as in large. They often began as grass-roots movements, although often in large towns; records by new musicians would be sold in one record store servicing a small area. The best example is the sale of Elvis Presley's first record, in the area near where he went to high school.

Therefore, rock and roll surfaced after the shift from rural to urban blues, which served as its basis, and then went through its own form of change from rural to urban, regional to national. Before it became a major force in music, it had to move from the rural-urban pattern to a local-regional-national pattern, centered around commercialization and marketing.

In other words, rock and roll began as a rough form of music (somewhat like the rural blues of the late nineteenth century), became an urban blues form, and then eventually embraced other forms in order to expand the market. Commercialization led to the free acculturation discussed previously, and consequently the significance of the shift from rural to urban became somewhat less important. It is an explanation rather than a complete description of what actually happened.

Ballads

We will discuss the actual style of ballads in the section on crooners, but we must first take up the issue of why ballads were significant in the late 1950s. The way the ballad expanded the listening audience was extremely important in broadening the form and gaining general acceptance by the public.

The first rock and roll ballads predate the invention of the term *rock and roll*. "Ol' Man River" by the Ravens in 1947 is usually considered part of the history of rhythm and blues, but this tune is essentially a ballad — a slow song with a structure based on two themes (theme 1, theme 1, theme 2, theme 1). The AABA form, as it can also be represented, is a basic ballad form. Many of the "bird" groups and later imitators sang slow songs in the ballad tradition (sometimes copying Frank Sinatra). These ballads, done in a style considered to be black, were very slick compositions. They usually featured a lead singer with a backup vocal group, sometimes with relatively complex harmonies.

By 1956 or 1957, there was in the United States a return to dancing, which had become a somewhat lost art after the demise of the big bands.

However, this time dancing was for the young, probably as a result of their leisure time and relative affluence. Rock and roll was the kind of music they wanted at dances, and the five types of songs discussed earlier were the ones played.

A party which lasts even an hour has some logical guidelines concerning what music is selected. Contrast is the key word in the successful selection of music; with even the most homogeneous of groups, it is necessary to provide different kinds.

The most diverse crowd of people to choose music for is probably one attending a large reception. In the 1980s people will ask for everything from the Average White Band to Flatt and Scruggs. People at large receptions range in age from two to ninety, and this makes music selection challenging. There has to be a little something for everyone, and it is necessary to have contrast, like a fast song followed by a slow one. If only fast rock and roll or only slow ballads from the 1940s were played, the people would get bored.

The same was true in the 1950s, when dancing became so popular. Although the crowds were less diverse (especially at school dances), their needs for changes in tempo and mood were just as precise. The market required different types of songs, which is one of the reasons why five different types emerged, all equally important.

Ballads were significant as elements of contrast, for relaxing the tension of rock and roll shouters. They also spoke to a larger audience because they were based on an earlier tradition. Although they often had quite uninspiring lyrics, as did many of the popular ballads of the 1940s, they were relaxing and they were pretty.

Also, ballads were used for a particular kind of dancing which was very popular in the 1950s. Some of the dance styles associated with faster music were fairly complicated and frankly acrobatic, but slow dancing was something anyone could do. The bop, the twist, and even the hokey-pokey required some expertise. Slow dancing was often called the "hug-and-squeeze" approach. The male and the female simply held on to each other, moving their feet back and forth or not at all.

The significance of the ballad in the years 1956 to 1959 was major. It expanded the range of music for rock and roll musicians and the size of their audience.

ANALYSIS OF TOP SONGS

In this section, we will use information from *Billboard's* "Number One Hit" to trace the emergence of rock and roll as a pop phenomenon. Of course, this is not the only method we could use to determine the effect of rock and roll, but it will give some indications of patterns of popularity.

In 1950 the top single on January 7 was Gene Autry's "Rudolph the Red-Nosed Reindeer." In February, the Andrews Sisters had the top spot. In July, Nat King Cole took over with "Mona Lisa," which was straight crooning. In 1951, Patti Page had the top song, "Tennessee Waltz," in January and February, followed by Perry Como, Les Paul and Mary Ford, Nat King Cole again, Tony Bennett, and Rosemary Clooney; the year ended with Johnny Ray's "Cry."

In 1952 and 1953 the trend continued, with Patti Page coming out on top.

Most of the songs popular in the early 1950s were either ballads (sung by crooners) or novelty tunes. They were aimed strictly at white audiences and not at the young.

Eddie Fisher, Doris Day, and Perry Como started 1954, which is consistent with previous trends. However, in the first week of August, "Sh-Boom" by the Crewcuts was number one. This particular tune was probably the first rock-and-roll-oriented tune to become number one, although a careful listening will reveal virtually no rock and roll characteristics, at least none that would have been so defined at that time. However, this was the kind of lyric which would become the staple of rock and roll ballads in the late 1950s. "Mr. Sandman" by the Chordettes held the top position in December 1954.

In July 1955 Bill Haley made it to the top with "Rock Around the Clock," remaining there for eight weeks. Mitch Miller (who still professes a dislike for rock and roll) took over from the Comets with the "Yellow Rose of Texas." "Love is a Many-Splendored Thing" by the Four Aces followed; and at the end of the year Tennessee Ernie Ford made it to the top with "Sixteen Tons," interestingly the kind of lyric which could work in rock and roll, although in this setting it was a standard ballad.

"Memories Are Made of This" put Dean Martin on top for the first time in 1956; Martin was one of the great crooners of the 1950s, although he was never involved with rock and roll. Kay Starr was number one on February 18 with "Rock and Roll Waltz," which is a rather strange hybrid. Elvis Presley was first with "Heartbreak Hotel" in April, and he dominated the top spot for the next two years. Guy Mitchell made it briefly with "Singing the Blues" at the end of 1956; Tab Hunter, Pat Boone, Perry Como, and Paul Anka all held the top spot briefly in 1957 with ballads.

Novelty tunes had a banner year in 1958 with "Witch Doctor," "Purple People Eater," "Hang Down Your Head, Tom Dooley," and "The Chipmunk Song." One of the great ballads of the 1950s, "Venus" by Frankie Avalon, was number one in 1959, as well as "Lonely Boy" by Paul Anka. The year 1960 saw the reemergence of Presley and continued success of such novelty tunes as "Alley-Oop" and "Itsy Bitsy Teenie Weenie Yellow Polka-Dot Bikini."

The dance phenomenon of Chubby Checker was introduced in 1961, first with "Pony Time" on February 27, but 1962 was really the big year for twist tunes. On October 20, the last great monster song made the top — "Monster Mash" by Boris Pickett and the Crypt Kickers. This song was reintroduced in the 1970s and was again successful. In 1961 and 1962, Ray Charles was on top several times, but never for what I consider to be the best tune of the 1950s, "What'd I Say?"

The Beatles dominated from the year 1963, but the charts took on a different character. The kinds of songs seen by looking at the entire list from 1950 to 1962 give one view of rock and roll. What happened after that is quite different.

MAJOR PERFORMERS

In this section, we will consider eighteen different performers, grouped under the different types of songs previously discussed. Some of the musicians will receive more coverage than others, mainly because they produced more music and/or were more important. (Ray Charles will be treated as a separate category.) It should be remembered that these are only examples and that there are other musicians who are undoubtedly as important or more so.

Rhythm and Blues

In this section we will consider Chuck Berry, Sam Cooke, King Curtis, and Bo Diddley. Berry and Diddley were great guitar players, at least by the standards of the 1950s; Cooke was an influential singer and bluesman; and Curtis was probably the best saxophone player of the 1950s in rhythm and blues (not counting jazz musicians). These men were known mainly for their contribution to rhythm and blues as it was associated with rock and roll.

Chuck Berry was the most influential of the four in that many other musicians copied his style; he continued to be an influence in the 1960s — on the Beatles and the Rolling Stones among others — and 1970s. He was a seasoned veteran by the mid-1950s, which placed him in a somewhat enviable position. Like Bill Haley, he combined country and western and rhythm and blues. However, as a black musician, he had perhaps a better feel for the rhythm and blues part and was a substantially better guitar player. Many people also believe that he was a better performer.

Careful listening to some of his songs from different eras will illustrate that his lyrics were aimed at youth, although they were somewhat more sophisticated than those of other musicians of the time. Many of his songs were not accepted as real classics until years after he had first performed them. "Surfin' U.S.A." had a different title originally; Brian Wilson added the words and turned this one song into a model for surfing music. Both the Beatles and the Rolling Stones sang Berry tunes, and they were successful with them.

More important is the fact that Berry was an excellent technician, that is, a technically good guitar player, which was unusual in the 1950s. Of the big stars, Bill Haley was a competent country and western guitarist but mainly in the chordal style. Elvis Presley could strum chords on the guitar but was lost when it came to playing melodic lines. Berry could play melodically and quite quickly. He was also a capable improvisor and was definitely the model for the guitar soloists of the 1960s, even the acid rock musicians.

Berry used a riff orientation in his improvisations that came directly from the rhythm and blues tradition. He used the guitar as a complement to his voice, filling in passages at the end of a phrase. But more important, he used the guitar as a solo instrument to break up the vocal domination, as well as expressively to communicate the strength of the song. Although other musicians may have used the guitar visually, Berry combined visual uses of the instrument (stage presence) with playing well.

Berry has changed some over the years, although he retains his rocker roots, going back to the song "I'm a Rocker." He has gotten more technical in his playing; he uses more electronic devices; and the language of his songs updates the slang usages and subjects. His playing and singing are a constant source of energy and he continues to play what most musicians feel is very solid, or "good," rock and roll.

Sam Cooke was a tremendously important singer, although he died at a young age in 1964 (he was shot). His style is difficult to pin down because many of his important hits were in fact not backed up by traditional rhythm and blues or rock and roll ensembles. His first release in 1957 was called "You

Chuck Berry in 1959 *(United Press International Photo)*

Sam Cooke *(Courtesy of RCA Records)*

(Courtesy of Capitol Records)

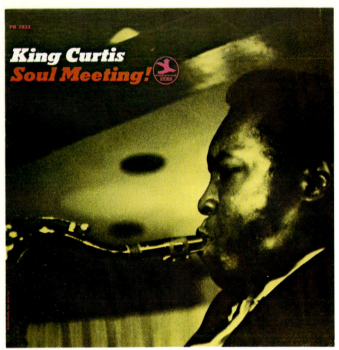
(Courtesy of Prestige Records)

(Courtesy of Columbia Records)

(Courtesy of Columbia Records)

(Courtesy of Columbia Records)

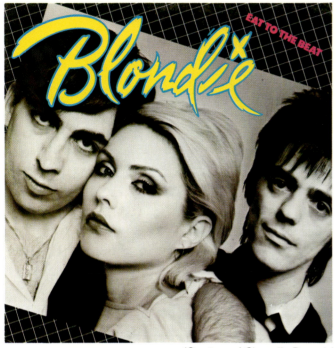

(Courtesy of Chrysalis Records)

(Courtesy of Prestige Records)

(Courtesy of Chrysalis Records)

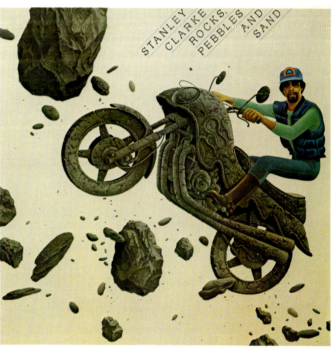

(Courtesy of Columbia Records)

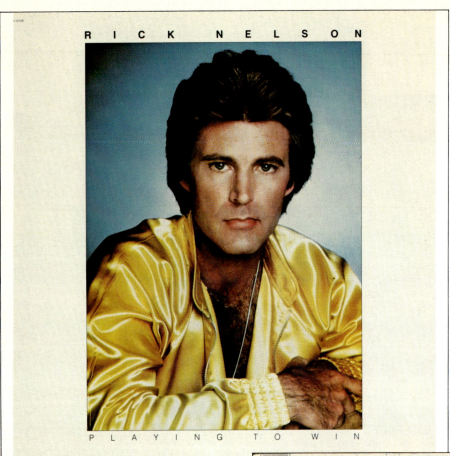

(Courtesy of Capitol Records)

(Courtesy of Columbia Records)

Send Me." His records (over seven years) were mainly of pop tunes, many of them slow songs in a crooning style. In the fast tunes (most of which were released in the 1960s) he revealed rhythm and blues roots, especially in vocal inflection.

However, in public performances Cooke revealed completely his ties to the blues. He had a relatively "clean" voice, in the sense that he was a pure singer. He had an excellent range, very good control, and a fine rhythmic feel. He did not shout at his audience, although he was a good interpreter of the style. Had his career lasted longer or had it been at a different time, he undoubtedly would have recorded fewer pop tunes. Cooke was an important figure in the soul movement, although he did not live long enough to grow with it.

King Curtis was mentioned in Chapter Two as one of the most significant saxophonists in the shouting classification. In fact, he was probably the best saxophonist in that tradition because of pure technical virtuosity; he had a full tone, played a lot of notes, and had a very melodic style. Most saxophonists of the 1950s played stereotyped solos, which were basically the same thing over and over. Curtis came from the jazz tradition and riff orientation of rhythm and blues. Thus, he was able to string together long melodic phrases within the rhythm and blues style. Had he chosen the way of John Coltrane he might have become one of the jazz greats. However, his significance is in rhythm and blues and in his playing strength.

Many of Curtis' tunes were blues numbers, and he was also influential in the soul movement. He had his share of pop crossover tunes and was a continuing example for other saxophone players, many of whom copied his big sound. He played a great deal of jazz, often with a small jazz quartet. Although known primarily as a tenor player, he also played excellent soprano saxophone. He died in 1971.

Bo Diddley (Elias McDaniel) was a rhythm and blues musician of stature in the early 1950s, and in fact, was one of the major performers in Alan Freed's Rhythm and Blues Extravaganzas. As a guitar player, he ranked in importance with Chuck Berry, although his playing was quite different. Whereas Berry had tremendous ability at melodic improvisation, Diddley played with a rhythmic vitality which was unparalleled. In fact, he had what was called the "Bo Diddley Beat." He pioneered the intelligent use of the electric guitar, in his case a solid electric guitar (not the acoustic construction). He set the controls on his guitar and amplifier (more on this topic in Chapter Ten) to achieve a deep, guttural sound. The tone, full of distortion and sounding almost dirty, had great influence on guitar players throughout the 1970s. This was really a rather remarkable innovation at a time when technology did not really provide many alternatives. An especially good recording to listen to is *Two Guitars*, featuring both Berry and Diddley. Diddley's improvisation tends to be more chordal in orientation than Berry's, but he plays with a very solid feel. He had widespread influence in the 1950s and 1960s.

Shouters

Although there were hundreds of shouters in the 1950s, we will consider only four of them: Duane Eddy, Buddy Holly, Jerry Lee Lewis, and Little Richard. Although they may have played in the rhythm and blues format, these musicians are called shouters because they were primarily known for their strength and/or loud songs.

Duane Eddy was a country-rock guitar player with a very distinctive sound. He was known as a twanger because of the way he strummed the guitar (letting it ring after hitting a chord). Many of his recordings were in fact made in the 1960s, but they were made in a 1950s style. Eddy really played the same way as Bo Diddley, although most of his songs were not blues tunes at all but rather strong pop tunes. He made a surfing album; backed up Nancy Sinatra in her famous song, "Boots"; and was a popular forerunner of some of the important guitar players of the 1960s. He is discussed in this section because he played in a very strong way, and he popularized what other musicians did somewhat earlier.

Buddy Holly might certainly have been as important to the history of rock and roll as Presley was, had he only lived longer. His career lasted only from 1956 to 1959. Born in Lubbock, Texas, he was at first a country musician, switching to rock and roll in the last part of 1956. Between 1957 and his death on February 3, 1959, he recorded a great number of hits, both his own songs and the music of others. Some of his most important tunes were "Peggy Sue," "That'll Be the Day," "Early in the Morning," "Shake, Rattle and Roll," "Blue Suede Shoes," and "Rip It Up." He died in a plane crash with Richie Valens and the Big Bopper (mentioned later).

Holly, who could also be discussed as a crooner, was similar to Elvis Presley in some ways. The major difference between them was that Holly's country roots, and therefore his vocal inflections, were Southwestern, or "Tex-Mex." He was capable of using extreme contrast in his voice in order to create different moods, and although he did not have the range or probably the native talent of Presley, his performances took advantage of all his technique. He was not an extremely good-looking person, although at the height of his career he was made to look pretty good. He personified a rebel image on stage and became the center of attention, overshadowing his group, the Crickets. He had a protruding Adam's apple, which was probably a focus for attention.

What was significant about Holly was his image of rebellion, and as a performer he elicited sympathy from the crowd. As he seemed to be going through real pain while he was performing, those present also felt it and had to be affected by it. Audience identification was high, not because Holly performed to entertain but because of the image he carried through his performances. At the time of his death, he was second in popularity to Presley. For some people, Buddy Holly was and still is a cult figure; also some people feel he was the real central figure of rock and roll in the 1950s.

Jerry Lee Lewis was a contemporary of Presley and was in many ways an imitator. Originally from Louisiana, he combined country and western with rhythm and blues. He was a piano player, and he put the same kind of energy into playing the piano that Presley did into playing the guitar. His most popular song was "Great Balls of Fire" in 1957, recorded in the same Memphis studio that gave Presley his start. He toured England in the late 1950s and failed miserably, primarily because of public scandal over his thirteen-year-old wife. He made a comeback in the late 1960s mainly as a country and western performer.

Lewis's style was straight shouting. He pounded the keyboard, used his fists and arms, and screamed at the audience. He sang a number of the same tunes that Presley did, but he usually recorded only the fast ones. Most of the songs were fast blues progressions (jump blues) which fit his technique the best. Although successful as a rock and roll shouter, he did not show Presley's versatility nor was he managed as well. His image was certainly right for a

Buddy Holly   *(Photo copyright © William F. Griggs. Used by permission)*

Jerry Lee Lewis *(Used by permission of Fred Reif, Black Kettle Records, Saginaw, Michigan)*

rock and roll star, but within a relatively limited spectrum. He simply did not combine enough musical elements to become the kind of star Presley was.

Little Richard (Richard Penniman) was and still is the king of the screamers. He was born in Macon, Georgia, in 1935, and unlike some of the other musicians mentioned, grew up totally within the rhythm and blues context. He had a heavy dose of gospel singing in his youth, and as a young teenager he turned to blues shouting, ultimately hitting it big with "Tutti Frutti" in 1955 (a million-record seller). From 1955 to 1957, he was constantly on top, running a close second to Presley. In 1957 he quit singing and performing completely for religious reasons, but in the early 1960s he returned to the music scene, first through gospel and then back to rock and roll. In performance, he never failed to show that in the shouting style, he was the best. He probably outdid Presley in this style and certainly led to the early demise of Bill Haley's popularity.

Little Richard was a piano player, although probably not a great one. He had no inhibitions at all, either in singing or playing. He wore baggy suits and outlandish clothes, but his main claim to fame was his hair, styled in a high pompadour. Some people have called him the Muhammed Ali of the 1950s, which is an apt comparison. His image was that of an antihero. He gave off great electricity in performances, and he was a constant bundle of energy. His songs were fast blues progressions, in which the lyrics were relatively meaningless. His stage presence was all-consuming, and he used whoops, slides, drop-offs, and screams. Little Richard belongs on any list of classic rock screamers.

Crooners

The crooners came mainly from the north, or more properly said, from the white tradition. We have stated that crooning was essentially started by white singers, going back as far as Rudy Vallee, and that black musicians adapted the style to their own form of pop music in the late 1940s. The crooners of the late 1950s were white performers, and this particular style of singing was clearly aimed at a white audience.

In the 1950s, it was easy to call the shouters rock and roll musicians, but the crooners were hard to classify. We consider them to be part of rock and roll, but that belief is at least debatable. However, these songs were performed partially for the rock and roll audience, at least insofar as that means young people. Crooning songs, or ballads, relied on the following basic characteristics:

1. a clearly recognizable, charismatic singer;
2. a slow and dreamy lyric, often about a simple emotion;
3. a slow, continuous background of instruments and/or vocal group;
4. a rhythmic feel, which often broke up the measure into twelve beats (four groups of three);
5. an attempt to characterize life as happy.

Whereas many of the rhythm and blues and shouting tunes were critical and/or pessimistic, ballads were almost always optimistic. In some ways, the history of the ballad is a more precise social indicator than other types of rock and roll.

A few of the crooners mentioned started their careers before what we will call the "golden age of slow songs" (roughly 1957 to 1960), but these tunes were sung more extensively at this time. That is, although previously musicians could get by singing just fast tunes, by 1957 they had to have contrast ballads in order to survive. Again, the movement toward dancing (with the development of particular dance steps) probably had more to do with this development than any other single factor.

As the movie industry capitalized with Elvis Presley on the romantic view of life, the recording and performing industries capitalized on the pretty faces of white northern crooners in their attempt to capture large markets, including middle-class America. Marketing and commercialization undoubtedly had a great deal to do with the rise of slow songs, but so did the attitudes of society. American life in the late 1950s can be seen cynically as the lull before the storm of the 1960s, but it could also be viewed as a relaxed and comfortable era.

In this section we will consider the following singers: Paul Anka, Frankie Avalon, Pat Boone, Dion and the Belmonts, Fabian, Ricky Nelson, and Tommy Sands. There are of course many others who could be considered, but these performers are a good cross-section of this type.

Paul Anka, white, originally from Canada, achieved tremendous success. In 1958 he had his first hit tune, "Diana," which sold nine million copies; he was fifteen at the time. A prolific composer, he wrote well over two hundred songs in the next five years and was a self-made millionaire by the time he was twenty-one. From the very beginning he had a natural ability to meet people and to act appropriately in front of audiences. He became a leading power in the music industry because of his shrewd business sense.

Anka, who had an extremely beautiful voice, was a classic crooner. As a teenage idol, he was cute, smiled a lot and was the darling of women, especially women who were older than he was. His songs spoke of love, embracing, and other images which fit well with dancing. He was definitely a pop musician in that he spoke to a wide audience, much surpassing the audience solely associated with rock and roll and/or rhythm and blues. His performances in public, for instance Las Vegas, were packed, and he appealed to a wide spectrum of society. Anka was a perfect model for the kind of phenomena described in the ballad era, and he was one of the leaders; he also continued to be popular over time.

Frankie Avalon is another good example of the young musician who has a big success with one song and then continues to be popular, although he did not continue to be a major force like Paul Anka; however, he did have nostalgia value, even after the Beatles became popular. Avalon was originally a trumpet player, and his first big hit was "Venus" in 1959. He was in the movies in the beach-party format and continued to produce hit tunes until roughly 1964. He had a beautiful voice and was quite attractive.

The most important thing about Avalon was probably the lyrics of his songs and the way that he sang them. As a singer, he was a romantic crooner without any awesome stage technique; he just presented beautiful songs. His lyrics were packed with images of love (mostly love at a distance), and he was a symbol of man reaching out to woman (or vice versa). "Venus" was a verse and refrain song, with contrast between the musical presentations of the two parts; the verse had a light-textured rock beat, and the refrain had more of a swing beat. It was efficient music without too much complexity; but it was technically well done and was quite successful.

Pat Boone had an enormously successful career which he passed on to one of his children, Debby Boone. Although some people may question his inclusion in a book on rock and roll, his popularizations of rock and roll hits were significant. Boone performed other people's music, not his own, and changed it so it would be palatable to a large audience. He was known for religious songs, renditions of old standards, and cover versions of rhythm and blues tunes. In this last context he was quite important, although he must always be considered a crooner.

Although Boone was criticized by people on both sides of the issue, he

Paul Anka in concert, 1981 *(Photo by Barry Rankin)*

legitimized rock and roll by making it popular with nonrock audiences. He stood for strong Christian values, was a representative of white middle-class America, and presented a clean-cut image. To those who supported that position, his singing of rock and roll was questionable. To those who supported other values, he was an inappropriate spokesman; they would have preferred to have someone more within the tradition singing their songs. When he did "Ain't That a Shame," originally by Fats Domino, and other songs from the rhythm and blues repertoire, he offended the purists who would have wanted the original artist to get the credit and the money. However, for the audience that liked the song no matter what its source, Boone presented a version of a song which might not have been accepted had it been sung by the original black artist.

The important point is how Boone changed these original tunes and what the resultant sound was. He sang in a pure voice without any of the blues inflections of rhythm and blues singers. The background sound was more swing beat or big band in orientation than rock and roll. He sang fast tunes in medium speed with a smooth and mellow voice. He took the hardness out of fast songs, and he took the mushy emotionalism out of slow songs. In essence, he watered down the sound as well as the lyrics. Although white proponents of the rhythm and blues tradition before Boone (Haley and Presley) had watered down the lyrics slightly, they still retained the rhythmic and emotional intensity of the originals. Boone watered down those elements as well. In this sense, he was a crooner even when he sang rhythm and blues tunes.

Dion and the Belmonts, with Dion DiMucci as the leader, represented a particular tradition within this era. In 1960, this group emerged with "teenage" songs, that is, songs specifically aimed at a teenage audience, and often with the word "teenager" (or "teen") in the title. In 1961, the group made the top of the charts with "Runaround Sue." Some of their important songs were "Teenager in Love," "Teen Angel," and "Lonely Teenager." They were one of the first groups to perform what would later be called "bubble gum music."

The Belmonts were all of Italian descent — DiMucci, D'Aleo, Milano, and Mastrangelo — and the vocal sound was high pitched and very emotional. It was plaintive, reminding some people of a weak version of Italian opera. There was a definite rock and roll feel to the music, but it was light rock. The instrumental backing was generally simple, and the focal point was the lyric and the sound of the voices. The lyrics were clearly aimed at teenagers, particularly young teenagers. The tunes tended to be sung at medium speed and had little improvisation or technical virtuosity. Although their audience was quite specific, it was also quite lucrative. We might be tempted to dismiss this group as not very interesting, but "teen rock" is a big business, and at least one example should be mentioned.

Fabian (Fabiano Forte), also of Italian descent, was essentially groomed as a Presley look-alike. When a major artist was successful, there were always attempts to capitalize on this success by patterning other people after the same model. This had happened with the "bird" groups in the late 1940s, and it happened again with Elvis Presley. Fabian was signed by a record company when he was thirteen years old and was literally made into a rock and roll star. His one hit song, "Tiger," in 1959 seemed to have justified this experiment. However, he was to have little impact in future years.

Fabian was and still is an extremely good-looking man. His long hair, dark skin, and strong body made him a natural sex symbol. Ultimately getting into pictures, with John Wayne in "North to Alaska" and in less notable beach-party films, he was successful in the image he was presenting. However, his style only worked at that time and did not endure the changes of the 1960s. Fabian is occasionally mentioned on television record ads, but his career is now obscure.

Although Fabian at times tried to emulate the great shouters, he was primarily a crooner in the softer rock and roll tradition. He was most at home in the emotional kind of song performed for the beach-party set. He was not endowed with a tremendous voice, but as Stan Freeberg pointed out in his parody on rock musicians, that was really not necessary. What he exuded was good looks, and during his period of success, that sufficed.

Ricky Nelson is an interesting case because he was popular before he became a singer. As the younger son on the famous "Ozzie and Harriet" television show, he was simply the cute kid who did normal boyish things. However, as the show got older, and the characters along with it, Ricky Nelson began to become popular with preteens and then ultimately teenagers. His singing career began on the television show and was then marketed in the Presley tradition. Fan clubs were formed all over the world, and by 1959 Nelson was an important entertainer. His greatest successes occurred between 1959 and 1964, before the Beatles became popular. One record, "Travelin' Man," hit the top in 1961.

Although he consciously patterned himself after Presley, especially his body motions and sneer, Nelson was really much more of a crooner or soft rock performer. He appealed to a wide audience, but most of his records were sold to young teenagers. He was a good singer and made a serious comeback in 1969; as a seasoned performer he was very good with audiences. The television show and his recording career went together, sort of like that of the Partridge family. It was a neat package, and it fit the marketing techniques of that period.

Tommy Sands is another Presley imitator who was fairly popular in the late 1950s. Although best known as the person who married Nancy Sinatra, he was important as a singer of young teenage songs, definitely in the crooning tradition. Examples of his songs are "Teenage Crush" and "Cutie Wootie." In some ways, his career and characteristics were interchangeable with some of the other musicians mentioned here. He was in the films of the time, he was good-looking, and he sang moderately well within the style.

Specialty Songs

Specialty songs either discuss some specific topic or use some special set of words in a very distinctive way. Clearly, tunes associated with some new dance step could be considered specialty songs. We specify these as a separate category because there is something about each particular song which has nothing to do with its style. That is, there is one thematic idea or some element of music which is special. In some ways, the next category, monster songs, is a subclass of this one.

The most significant kind of special technique is some unusual voice quality. If the voice quality is the single important thing about the tune, we would consider that to be a specialty tune. Any composition which uses a special voice quality throughout the whole piece is *not* a specialty tune, because that voice quality becomes the style of the piece. However, if a group

Rick Nelson *(Courtesy of Capitol Records)*

uses a particular sentence or voice quality once or twice in a composition, it will be considered distinctive.

Many of the "bird" groups mentioned previously used a low bass voice as an element of contrast, which would make them specialty songs. One particular example is the line, "Why is everybody always picking on me?" from the Coasters' "Charlie Brown." These phrases often take on some narrating quality in the sense that they express the real emotional and lyrical content of the whole song. Most rock and roll songs speak from a point of view of total communication and do not express much of what the performer really wants to say. When a performer reveals him- or herself or something about a character, it is unique and often occurs through these special devices.

J. P. Richardson (known as the Big Bopper) used one line consistently in his performances and recordings. It was simply, "this is the Big Bopper speaking." His only major hit was "Chantilly Lace" in 1958, an up-tempo song about a particular girl. Very popular at the time, but different from other tunes, it communicated through the medium of the Big Bopper. Although it was undoubtedly a clever piece, what was important was the autobiographical nature of the narrating function. Had Big Bopper not been killed in the same plane crash with Buddy Holly and Richie Valens, he might have continued this concept over the years. As rock musicians began to see themselves as communicators of significant and major ideas, the tendency to use the first person would become greater.

Chubby Checker was a specialty song performer, and it is easy to explain why. He was a rhythm and blues piano player and frankly an excellent musician. His roots go back to the stride pianists previously mentioned. However, his career would have been insignificant had it not been for the twist. In 1960 he recorded the "Twist," a composition by Hank Ballard, and the dance craze took off. The twist was popular with different kinds of people, and it even enjoyed great success in Europe. Although the music was good, the only important thing about it was the dance step associated with it — which is why it was a specialty song.

The last musician we will discuss in this section is Fats Domino, who is special because of a particular thing he does with his voice. He sings with a throat growl which gives his music a very special flavor. Many people tried to imitate this sound, but somehow Domino is the only one who can do it. There are many good things about his music, but the throat growl makes it special.

We should not assume that because musicians have been placed in one category or another that they were incapable of singing or did not sing in other styles as well; we have placed them where they were most influential. The musicians who have been placed in this category were involved in other styles as well, but they did one thing which made them unique, and people especially enjoyed them for that reason.

Monster Songs

Monster songs are really a subclass of novelty tunes, of which there were many in the period under consideration. Novelty songs are present in every era of music. Examples from the big-band era include the arrangement of the "Woody Woodpecker Song" in which the instruments imitate the sound of a woodpecker, and the train effect at the beginning of Glenn Miller's "Chattanooga Choo-Choo." Novelty songs are catchy, and they rely on some special image to attract attention. We mention monster songs here because they seem to be a rather nice model, especially for musicians who would have been otherwise unknown.

The idea of monsters is, interestingly enough, attractive to rock musicians. Certainly the *Yellow Submarine* of the Beatles incorporates the idea of monsters, in this case, evil monsters who set out to keep the world from having music. The monster image in the Who's *Tommy* and the blatant monsters of Kiss or other punk groups are quite apparent. However, the monsters in the 1950s were somewhat less evil; they were benevolent monsters who were not to be taken seriously. As such, they were slightly more redeeming characters, ludicrous at times, but always entertaining.

Two songs from this era with rather attractive monsters were "Purple People Eater" by Sheb Wooley in 1958 and "Monster Mash" by Boris Pickett and the Crypt Kickers in 1962. The first monster was a happy little fellow who came to visit and wanted to stay. He flew but was not really dangerous; he was cute. The "Monster Mash" was a dance step, and again the monster image was benevolent. These tunes were up-tempo pop songs designed to hit the charts quickly. They both did so and then became collector's items. Monster records are still occasionally produced, bringing together fifteen or twenty of the most successful songs of the genre.

RAY CHARLES

This chapter ends with a discussion of the impact of Ray Charles, a transition figure between the 1950s and 1960s. Although he may not have achieved the fame or the money of other musicians, he is a pivotal figure in the history of rock and roll, finishing the process of legitimizing the art form.

Ray Charles was born in Albany, Georgia, on September 23, 1930. His youth was spent in Greenville, Georgia, a small town near the Florida border. The story of his youth is extremely interesting, and anyone who wants to know more should definitely read his autobiography. To make a long and intriguing story fairly short, his early life was hard: When he was five he saw his brother drown, and he lost his vision when he was seven. His family was poor, uneducated, and downtrodden. Consequently, his development follows the pattern of the black blues singer, and many of the things said in Chapter Two apply here. Charles was originally in the blues tradition, and he came to rock and roll rather late, that is, in the late 1950s. He developed first as a rhythm and blues musician and gospel singer. By the early 1950s, he was a significant jazz musician. When he started doing rock and roll tunes at the end of the 1950s, he brought with him professionalism and experience in the recording industry. Many record producers, and musicians as well, have talked about how much Charles taught them, rather than the other way around.

Charles is an excellent pianist, a competent saxophone player, and a superb singer. As a blind musician, he evokes feelings that sighted musicians do not. Obviously he served as a model for little Stevie Wonder and for virtually every important black musician from the 1960s on. He was the first soul singer, and any discussion of Motown should start with him, even though he is a southerner.

Ray Charles *(Photo by Sherry Suris, Photo Researchers, Inc.)*

The style of Ray Charles is a combination of gospel and rhythm and blues, with some jazz elements thrown in. It is not basically rock and roll, but the resultant sound has been embraced as that of the late 1950s. As well as combining all these elements, he predates many pop and soul musicians in the use of larger instrumental ensembles. During the 1950s, he worked the rhythm and blues circuit with a distinctive style of singing.

He has a large vocal range, and uses call and response extensively, both between his voice and the backup musicians and between himself and the audience. He uses a shouting style reminiscent of strong gospel singers, and the players extensively imitate rhythmic riffs. He clearly combines elements of the profane (rhythm and blues) with the sacred (gospel).

By the end of the 1950s, Charles began working with a larger group of musicians, many of whom have gone on to become leaders in the jazz movement, in particular in Detroit. He used the larger ensemble as a responding unit to his singing, not wanting to be the whole production by himself. His piano playing served both as accompaniment to himself and also as part of the ensemble, which was somewhat unique. Many of his recordings from the late 1950s and early 1960s were technically superior to other recordings of black musicians, partly because of the superiority of his band and also because of his knowledge of recording techniques. He was demanding in his standards, although reports of that time indicate that he was a very easy person to work with because he was so professional.

He had difficulties with drugs in the 1960s but managed to surmount them; he also had difficulties with the law. He continued to perform and record in the 1960s and 1970s and is still quite active today. He is a consummate performer in many different styles and is a great credit to the profession.

Charles developed in a somewhat more complete way than any other musician considered in this book. At the school for the blind which he attended, he was given formal musical instruction, and by virtue of the time period of his formative years (early 1940s), he was schooled in the outside world in every kind of music. By the time he moved to Jacksonville, Florida, at the age of fifteen, he was already aiming for a career in music; however, unlike many other musicians in this book he did not catapult to fame overnight. He worked hard as a union musician, learning from the best and the worst, playing every kind of job imaginable. He copied other people's playing and learned to play whatever would get him work. As a result, he is able to move freely among blues, jazz, and any other kind of music imaginable. In this sense, Ray Charles is a complete musician.

A description of his entire recording and playing career would take at least one hundred pages because he has done so much. In his performing career, he has played with some of the best, starting as a young teenager with Cannonball Adderly. He played with other musicians who were already great, and he also allowed new musicians to play with him before their rise to stardom. Stevie Wonder performed with Charles as a sit-in musician when Wonder was ten years old. As an arranger, Charles made himself important to many of the ensembles in which he played; later he was the leader of his own band. His arranging technique was different than most because it was oral. He heard everything in his head and called out the right notes to be written down by the musician in charge of each part. In this history, Ray Charles is unique. No one else in the history of rock has quite his musical command.

His recording career is equally impressive; regardless of the period in his career, he was always in complete control of the musical forces. In the early 1950s, he was called on to produce the right sound for a specific need, both in his playing and singing, and also for the other musicians involved. He has always been the consummate studio musician because of his ability to adapt himself and to understand the roles of the other musicians. His early career provided the necessary tools; he was always interested in the imitative process and being able to do everything. Most rock musicians tend to have a relatively narrow approach to their role in the performing ensemble; Charles adapts himself to whatever is being done at the moment. He is equally at home in a jazz setting, in a rhythm and blues ensemble, or in classical music.

Each of his major hits (and sometimes tunes which did not become popular) illustrates mastery of style, flexibility, and technical precision. Charles was always ahead of the competition in the sense that each of his recorded performances was years ahead of the level of technology and complexity of the time in which it was actually produced. Even when he was producing race records, the technical level far surpassed that of other black artists. In this sense alone, Charles was a leader in his field.

The first tune we will consider is from 1955 — "I've Got a Woman." Although the lyrics seem to fit the model of a shouter, the instrumental backing does not. The ensemble is a straightforward jazz or rhythm and blues group: piano, bass, drums, and saxophone. The song has a number of short verses, although it is not a blues progression — it just sounds like it. His singing style is blues-oriented and features quite a bit of shouting. However, there is a tenderness about the way he sings, and he uses dynamic contrast to make the lyrics more effective. He employs call and response and also what we call *stop-time*, where he sings a short phrase by himself (without accompaniment) and the instruments respond; then he returns to the standard format. This particular device derives from gospel music and is a trademark of Charles' style. Probably the most significant contribution of this technique is audience involvement, which the trait will eventually evoke.

"Hallelujah, I Love Her So," which came out in 1956, is truly unique in the history of rock and roll and pop music of the 1950s. It uses a small big band as an extension of the instrumental ensemble in the earlier recording. The band is riff-oriented, which probably goes back to some of Charles' playing experiences and most certainly to his listening ones (Count Basie, Louis Jordan, and others). The lyrics, a combination of gospel and rhythm and blues, have religious as well as sexual overtones. Charles certainly loves women (many of them) and the lyrics of this particular song illustrate some of his feelings. There is a particularly attractive place where he sings about a woman knocking on the door; the drummer plays several repeated rim shots to suggest the knocking. We should always look for examples of this "word painting" in music.

A pivotal song in the history of rock and roll is "What'd I Say?", recorded in 1959. This song became almost a union card of sorts in the early 1960s. In order to get into any rock and roll band a musician had to be able to play the tune and to sing at least six verses of it. Much in the way that Charles had to be competent in a certain number of musical styles and songs in order to get work as a struggling musician, musicians now had to master his tune in order to get a job. This is a fitting tribute to Charles' struggle for success.

A fact we have not mentioned yet is that most rock and roll tunes from the 1950s were pretty short (two to three minutes in length). Most versions of "What'd I Say?" run about eight to ten minutes. This song is made up of very short lyric phrases (of eight measures); it is not a blues structure per se, although it is blueslike. It is really drawn from the old rural blues or primitive blues tradition. There is a refrain and there are many verses. The verses in the version on record are pretty clean, although they are obviously sexual in orientation. The verses in live performance are a bit more earthy.

The song begins and ends with audience participation. After singing many verses of the song, Charles stops. The audience starts responding, in a manner similar to gospel songs. He begins to respond to them and then finally breaks into a vocal utterance, which is repeated by the audience. This continues and builds, and then he breaks back into the song. He stops and starts it again. In this sense, he uses the audience like a rhythmic riff, building tension through repetition. This technique is based on rhythm and blues concepts, but in this piece, Charles uses all his talent — big-band backing, virtuoso piano playing, grunting, groaning, and audience participation. The sound of the song is simple but its overall structure is captivating.

This song is highly significant because it serves to bring together all the traditions of jazz, pop, and rock and roll. In a coherent way, Charles legitimizes rock and roll by adding jazz elements. With this one tune, he paves the way for further developments in rock and roll and ushers in the 1960s.

SUMMARY

Rock and roll in the 1950s was honest music, which communicated in simple terms. Because this is a chronological study we have the opportunity to sharpen our listening skills when the demands are not too great. As we progress through the history of this art form, listening will become difficult, especially in the more complicated styles.

The period of the late 1950s is often thought to be the dead time in rock and roll because there was some fairly undignified pop music in that era. We had lost the hard edge in rock and roll (or the way it was in the beginning). However, we should be able to see this period as part of the development of the form. It was becoming the communication medium of the general population, and it was also becoming big business.

The style in the last part of the 1950s capsulized everything that had happened in rock and roll. Although it may have lacked creativity in some ways, and some of the energy of the shouters had begun to wane, rock and roll made up for these losses by reaching out to many people. The marketing techniques and the sociological implications continued to be influential in the 1960s. Of course, we will see great changes in that decade, but this late period of rock and roll provides the basis for them. Later musicians return to the style of the late 1950s when they attempt to recapture the essence of rock and roll.

CHAPTER SIX

Attitudes of the 1960s

In this brief chapter, we will discuss those developments which ultimately were reflected in rock. In the following two chapters (Chapter Seven on the Beatles and Chapter Eight on California musicians) we will discuss musicians who were pivotal to that time. The Beatles were highly significant and disbanded just before the end of the decade; thus they are an excellent example. Some musicians who were really part of the 1960s will be discussed in connection with the following decade because their music led to some major phenomenon which had its major impact on the form at that time.

The 1960s reflected more intense change in the United States than any other time since the Revolutionary War. It is important to understand that many people were committed to the sense of change, committed in a way that perhaps they had never been before. Comprehending the depth of that commitment is imperative for a proper understanding of the art forms which sprang from it.

In the cycle of political change, the 1960s were Democratic years; that is, the Democratic party was in power. Like all cycles, it was probably a reaction to the Republican administration which had preceded it. The beauty of the American system is that it almost guarantees a slow shifting of power back and forth between progressive and conservative attitudes. The 1950s were basically conservative, and the 1960s were basically liberal. Political rhetoric always stresses the importance of moral and ethical philosophies, but in the 1960s the political ethic was based on philosophical values more than in other politically liberal times, for instance, in Franklin Roosevelt's administration.

The 1960s began with a new political image maker, John F. Kennedy, whose significance as a charismatic figure must not be understated. Kennedy represented a new dream for young Americans for many reasons. He was young; he had a beautiful wife; and he had young children. He was an Irish Catholic, and although he came from a powerful and rich family, he represented oppressed minorities. The Kennedy mystique was important, although we can objectively question how much substance it contained. Kennedy was handsome; he held crowds spellbound with his look and with his speech. He was the first media politician in the sense that he won a close race with Richard Nixon, many people believe, mainly on the basis of their famous television debates. The reason he won, say most analysts, is that he simply looked better and more statesmanlike. It is interesting that Nixon, in his triumphant return to politics in 1968, probably used television even better than Kennedy had. However, Kennedy used the media and some marketing techniques much as rock musicians would.

More than anything else, Kennedy gave faith to the American public, but a very different kind of faith than that of the 1950s. Let us remember that the 1950s were secure and prosperous for middle- and upper-class America. However, Kennedy suggested that it was time to spread that wealth to the rest of America and other parts of the world. He proposed a New Frontier, developments in outer space, the Peace Corps, and nuclear limitations. After becoming president, he did do quite a bit to promote international relations, and he became a world symbol for the oppressed. He was especially popular in Latin America (probably because he was Catholic).

In his inaugural address, he spoke of "passing the torch to a new generation of Americans," which although it may not have happened during his brief presidency, was at least a good symbol for the younger generation. When

Kennedy was shot in 1963, the entire world went into mourning. No matter how history will judge Kennedy as a president, he will remain symbolic of the 1960s.

There can be little doubt that the president responsible for real change in America was Kennedy's successor, Lyndon Johnson. Johnson was in effect the person to whom the mantle was passed. Kennedy's thoughts were to be translated into legislative action by Johnson, who really was more capable of controlling the politics of Congress. Johnson was personally responsible for most civil rights legislation and a score of governmental actions which serve as the legacy of the 1960s (social programs). Unfortunately, Johnson lost his credibility over Vietnam, but most historians will give him tremendous credit for his role in domestic changes.

Although Richard Nixon was elected president in the 1960s, he must be seen as a symbol for the end of that decade and the predictable swing to conservatism. The 1960s were energetic for a number of reasons, but by the end of the decade the movement was falling apart; the conservatives quickly took over.

One of the strong movements was the ecology movement, which began with Rachel Carson's book, *The Silent Spring*. Basically, the book was an argument against the proliferation of chemicals, which were destroying the delicate balance of nature. The ecology movement would become especially important by the mid-1960s, being almost synonymous with the hippie movement. Natural foods became the rage, a belief which carried over into the 1970s. Attitudes were progressive, and there was a curious trend toward simplifying life, which was basically what the ecology movement was all about.

Some of the interesting developments of the 1960s led to inventions; a good example is Buckminster Fuller's geodesic dome (an energy-efficient style of architecture). Ralph Nader's book, *Unsafe at Any Speed*, was a condemnation of American technology, although it was specifically aimed at the automobile industry. It was believed that technology must be controlled, or at least, must consider human needs.

Integration was a fundamental issue. Although theoretically integration began in the mid-nineteenth century, it was not until the 1960s that political action on a widespread basis had any effect. The black movement, riots over racial issues, and civil rights legislation (the Act of 1965) all pointed to the need for change within society. Although the black movement was first, it was quickly followed by other minority movements and ultimately by that for the Equal Rights Amendment.

Student demonstrations were focal points for change, first against the system and then against the Vietnam War. Students gained power within the system, and although there was ugliness which led ultimately to the massacre at Kent State University, there were some significant changes in students' rights. The importance of the student movement was that youth were demanding and getting responsibility. This demand ultimately would have an effect on rock, as a topic for lyrics and as a vehicle for changing its message.

The drug movement and the sexual revolution were important in the 1960s. The antiwar movement was also powerful and ultimately led to the end of President Johnson's administration. Some would argue that it significantly lowered the prestige of the United States. Even the image of professional athletes was affected, and for the first time our heroes became antiheroes — Joe Namath and Muhammad Ali, for example. Such figures garnered admiration because of their antisocial views rather than their all-American image.

    In conclusion, the 1960s were times of tumult and confusion. Establishment ethics were questioned, and people were committed to new ideas. The only value that seemed to be paramount was that of change. In my opinion, the 1960s represented the most compact historical change in the evolution of America. Even the Constitution was being questioned, that is, seriously questioned as opposed to reinterpreted. Rock music clearly had new messages, and fortunately the musicians popular during that time came up with new means to communicate the new values. The state of the art expanded, and the difference between rock and roll in the 1950s and rock in the 1960s is like night and day.

CHAPTER SEVEN

The Beatles

No book on rock and roll would be complete without a major discussion of the Beatles, for a number of reasons, although it is confusing that the most significant rock influence from the 1960s would be from England. Those tumultuous times had little effect on the Beatles themselves; in fact, they helped to produce some of the changes of the 1960s in the musical world. The Beatles is perhaps the only significant rock group whose entire history falls within that decade, even though, of course, it began in the late 1950s.

Our discussion of the Beatles will have two parts: biography and musical analysis. For the sake of brevity we will not repeat our previous analyses of stage techniques, marketing, and media expansion. For most of the groups from the 1960s on, such information is readily available either in books or magazines or as common knowledge.

BIOGRAPHY[1]

John Lennon (1940-1980) was born in Liverpool, England. His father, Fred, was employed on ships and had very little to do with his wife and son. His mother, Julia, did not in fact raise the boy; it was his Aunt Mimi who was given that task. His mother came into his life at various points; according to Hunter Davies, she was a bad influence.

Lennon was not good at school, although it is clear that he had intelligence. He was a rebel and a tough kid, and he dressed and acted like a Teddy boy, a British hoodlum. He was a juvenile delinquent, to put it in American terms. When he attended Quarry Bank High School in 1952, he quickly developed a reputation as a bad person.

It is important to realize that Lennon's life was a sad one. His father was nonexistent; his mother gave him up; and his Aunt Mimi's husband, George, died when Lennon was thirteen. He was in trouble at school, and although he was good at art, his artistic endeavors were not establishment-oriented. Although he ultimately went to art school, even that was not very satisfying. The only thing which ever led to anything concrete came out of a student gang he formed at Quarry High.

This group became musical only incidentally. Though it eventually included Paul McCartney and George Harrison, the initial group was simply a bunch of tough kids who hung around together. The interesting point, of course, is how they became musical, an event that occurred in the first part of 1956. To sum up the musicality of the Quarrymen in one word, it was primitive. Most of their music was of low quality and imitative. The musical style they imitated was called *skiffle*.

Skiffle has a fairly interesting history (see *Skiffle* by Brian Bird). The form derived from the United States as a combination of early rent-party music (described in Chapter One), country rhythm bands, Dixieland, and dance bands. Skiffle was "discovered" in England in the late 1940s and still thrives as a country kind of sound. It requires guitars, a bass instrument, miscellaneous percussion (like a washboard), and singing. The best analogy in the United States would be a jug band, which is normally associated with

---

[1]This biography relies rather heavily on information from the Hunter Davies biography. One might wish to consult Brian Epstein's *A Cellarful of Noise* or John Lennon's *Lennon Remembers*. For useful information on analysis of their music, one could use Wilfred Meller's *Twilight of the Gods: The Beatles in Retrospect* (New York: Viking Press, 1974).

country and/or folk music. At best, skiffle is simple music; at worst, it is just noise. What the Quarrymen produced would probably be classified near the bottom end of the spectrum.

The significance of skiffle can be traced through the early hits of the Beatles, although it can be heard primarily in the instrumental background. It has a continuous beat and is related only slightly to rock and roll. However, even a skiffle background can be used in back of a rock lyric. Many of the original Beatle tunes of the early era are in fact skiffle songs, and even the cover records of American rock and roll classics have a very different instrumental backing. Although this point is seldom made about English rock, there can be little doubt that skiffle was important, and its influence is one of the typically English characteristics — as opposed to the American ones — of rock.

The Quarrymen were of course inconsequential. While Elvis Presley was a star, the Beatles were still school kids and their music was no more than beating on garbage can lids. In 1956, John Lennon was sixteen and Paul McCartney was fourteen.

James Paul McCartney was born in Liverpool in 1942, the first son of Jim and Mary McCartney. The second son, Michael, was born in 1944. McCartney had a relatively cheerful childhood and seems to have had a close relationship with both his father and mother. As his parents were both musical, he learned some of his musicality at home. In particular, his father was in a dance band, and at several times did actually assist Paul and John. Paul's mother died when he was fourteen, and this most certainly had an effect on him.

McCartney was good at school, achieving higher academic success than the other Beatles. He was a prolific writer, and at the age of eleven he won an essay contest. He always had an interest in art and certainly could have become a professional artist. However, his mother's death seemed to turn him away from normal existence. His family continued to take care of the boys, but clearly things were rougher for them after the loss of their mother. His father bought him a guitar, and he spent much of his time learning to play it and experimenting. It was at this time that he became interested in American pop music, particularly Elvis Presley.

In the next two years, music became a dominant force in McCartney's life. The Beatles rose to musical fame from relatively austere beginnings. None of them were child geniuses, nor did they have formal training. Of any of them McCartney probably had the most help in music, primarily through his father. But to say that he was a phenomenal musician technically would be to overstate the issue. He experimented with very simple chord changes (progressions). It took him months to figure out the chord progressions of tunes that other musicians would grasp in fifteen minutes. His eventual fame probably came from his lyrics, his singing style, and his energy.

George Harrison, born in 1943 to Harold and Louise Harrison, was the youngest of four children. His family situation was happy and normal, and he grew to be an independent child. Davies' *The Beatles* points out that Harrison's mother was very important in his life because she was so supportive of whatever her children wanted to do. However, it was not until Harrison was fourteen that he showed any real interest in music.

In 1956 or 1957, he became interested in skiffle as an activity; the most important artist to him was Lonnie Donegan, who led a skiffle band. Again, the importance of skiffle was paramount as it led Harrison to develop some real talent in picking out tunes and in playing relatively complicated figures on the guitar. He started playing guitar at the same time as his older brother, Peter, and by the time he met Paul McCartney at the Liverpool Institute, he was an accomplished player, at least by comparison to McCartney. He eventually joined the Quarrymen in 1958, primarily because he was a better instrumentalist than either McCartney or Lennon. Over the years, Harrison made a lasting contribution to the Beatles from a technical perspective. Although he did not have the impact or visibility of McCartney and Lennon, many of the songs were in fact written around some chord change and/or melody he initially inspired.

The development of the Beatles from 1958 to 1962 is fascinating because we would be hard pressed to predict their achievement of any kind of success. They were basically a guitar group, and they remained skiffle-oriented. They added a drummer, Pete Best, who was important in establishing the group as a Liverpool institution. Best's mother ran a club called the Cavern, and this location became their home base.

They also went through a number of different musicians and different names for the group. Johnny and the Moondogs and the Silver Beatles were the most lasting, but there were many others. They were in the process of evolving from a skiffle band to a rock and roll band (English style). A concert tour of Scotland was frankly a failure, but they did several stints in Hamburg, Germany, in the early 1960s.

The year 1962 was important for the Beatles, as they had finally come to call themselves. Although they were still not the most important group in England, they had become quite competitive. They met their manager, Brian Epstein, during the last part of 1961; in 1962 they became associated with George Martin, who became their producer. In the late summer of 1962, they replaced Best with Ringo Starr, who at the time was more important, because of his popularity, than the other three put together.

By the fall of 1962, they were the center of British rock and had firmly established their particular style. They did a concert with Little Richard in October 1962, produced by Brian Epstein. Beatle mania was about to occur, if for a time only in England.

The years from 1962 to 1969 are probably best covered by the development of their music. However, it is important to realize that the Beatles were in their early twenties (George was nineteen) when they became successful. They were far from being mature individuals, psychologically or musically, and their career growth coincided with their personal growth. In some senses, their careers hindered their growth as people and in some ways it forced them to mature. Ultimately, the breakup in 1969 undoubtedly had something to do with their development as individuals.

Their personal relationships with one another are an interesting case. Any musical group develops a group identification because of the circumstances. The Beatles, like other groups in the making, literally lived with each other, even when they were still living at home. From 1956 until the mid-1960s, Lennon and McCartney were inseparable, being joined by Harrison in 1958. They spent a great deal of time with each other, even when the activities were not musical. However, they generated their musical identities by living them out with each other, much before the time when these would be successful performing techniques.

When they began playing engagements they did so as a group, traveling to and from the job together. They knew everything about each other, and as a result, they developed a sense of family. Even as the four of them began to marry and have separate family lives, they still remained the closest of friends. In fact, they were so close that their wives had difficulty breaking through to their husbands. Lennon's first marriage broke up, partially because of his inability to separate himself from the Beatles.

Ringo Starr was born in 1940 as Richard Starkey. His parents were divorced when he was three years old, and his mother remarried in 1953. His early life was rather tragic in that he had two major illnesses, both of which put him in the hospital for long periods. By his own admission he was very slow in school, and in fact could not read or write until he was eight or nine. To this day he has trouble with communication. He supposedly learned to play percussion instruments during his second hospital stay as a teenager. He rose to musical prominence by the time he was twenty-one, first through skiffle and then through pop music. Although he had no association with the Beatles, he was very popular by the time he finally joined them in 1962. In fact, some chroniclers have indicated that Starr was much more significant than the Beatles until 1962. His drumming style, although it was not flashy, was apparently right for the Beatles at that time.

The Beatles began to develop an international reputation with "She Loves You." Before coming to the United States, they also put out songs like "I Want to Hold Your Hand" and "Please, Please Me." The first album released in the United States was "Meet the Beatles," and by the end of 1963, they were quite successful here. (The style of these early tunes will be discussed later.) As a social phenomenon they were perhaps more interesting. They were foreigners, but it was precisely their foreignness which made them so captivating. They spoke with an obvious accent and their music was very different, even if it had certain structural similarities to American pop music. The lyrics of their songs fit the lyrical messages of the time. The songs were about girls, and in some ways, were really preteen songs in an English style. By this time, they had perfected their stage routine, but they had yet to be very innovative.

In February 1964, they came to the United States for a brief and successful maiden voyage. They were on the Ed Sullivan show and played at Carnegie Hall and in Washington, D.C. They were an instantaneous national success. Some critics have said that the timing was just right and that musically they really were not much good. However, the combination of the clothes, the Beatle "mop," and the foreign image was extremely successful because it was so well done. The marketing techniques were sophisticated, but even in their early era, they were awfully good at what they did. We can always take cheap shots at performers in earlier stages, criticizing their technique or the simplemindedness of their songs. However, we should remember that the Beatles were in their early twenties, they were trying to establish themselves, and they came from humble backgrounds. Had they not gone on to make such sweeping changes in the form, these criticisms might be valid. In view of the result, the criticisms are unjustified. Even in "Twist and Shout" the Beatles proved themselves showmen, and their basic energy in performance was significant even at the beginning.

They quickly followed this success with the production of their first film, "A Hard Days Night," which kept their popularity high (along with hit releases, of which there were many). The fact that the Beatles remained a British phenomenon was probably important in their tremendous popularity. Like Presley's stay in the army, it exuded a mystical quality for Americans. We could not touch the Beatles because they did not live here. Also important was the relative dearth of significant rock groups at that time. Although the Rolling Stones started in 1964, they were not to have a real impact until later (see Chapter Eleven).

During the summer of 1965, the Beatles returned to the United States for a second tour and were even more successful. The middle era of the Beatles really started after that tour, in which most of the concerts featured early tunes and a traditional Beatles look. Although they consciously avoided the comparison, they were certainly influenced by the rougher image of the Stones and Mick Jagger. *Help* was released in August, *Rubber Soul* in December, and *Revolver* in August 1966. These three albums are the most important releases of the middle era (1965–1966) and represent a slow change toward more complicated material. By this time, the Beatles were maturing as a musical group, and clearly their interests and their message were becoming more profound.

In 1966 they stopped touring, for several reasons. They were financially successful and did not need additional exposure. From this point on, they were strictly a studio and film group. The albums of the late period (*Sgt. Pepper's Lonely Heart's Club Band* in June 1967 through *Abbey Road* in October 1969) are true masterpieces in the history of rock. They illustrate a complexity of message and a profundity seldom found. The Beatles had gone full cycle by 1969, and their split was inevitable.

The breakup of the Beatles was undoubtedly caused by some of the following: (1) the end of group creativity, (2) a need for individual creativity, (3) personality conflict, (4) family pressures, (5) legal complications, and (6) financial necessity. We can argue for any or all of these causes. The group had accomplished so much in the evolution of its style (perhaps more than any other rock group), it is conceivable that there was nothing left. Also, both Lennon and McCartney had individual creative needs, which were not necessarily compatible. They had produced most of the songs together as a team. Obviously, as they began to grow, they also began to diverge. Their music during the 1970s illustrates a real difference, which probably existed before they split up.

Much has been made of the personality conflicts, and comments made after Lennon's death stress the influence of Yoko Ono. However, this particular allegation seems less convincing. It is obvious that the Beatles would begin to develop individual differences. After all, they were thirty years old. Although there was a need to establish independence, this in itself would not have been sufficient to dissolve the group.

Family pressures were very real. The fact that the Beatles developed different lifestyles is well documented. Certainly the pressures of their wives and growing families must have had something to do with breaking out on their own. Legal complications led to infighting, although we contend that this was incidental in comparison.

Finances probably had more to do with it than anything else. As a result of their phenomenal seven-year career as a group, they were all rich. The tax structure in England was such that intelligent financial planning was necessary in order to cope with this new-found wealth. Both the implications of having so much money individually and some fighting over the proper share of royalties were significant factors in creating a split. Each Beatle related to his new stature in life differently, and money was certainly at the bottom of it. Success was sweet for these poor lads from Liverpool, but when they achieved great wealth, they each had a different way of handling it.

Life for the Beatles after 1969 has been diverse. McCartney has been very active, although at first he retired to the country. His group, Wings, is quite excellent in its own right, and although he has settled into a middle-of-the-road kind of rock, he continues to have many admirers. Lennon was most productive lyrically, in conjunction with his wife, Yoko Ono. He became the most progressive of the Beatles, and although at times reclusive, he remained creative until his death. The other two Beatles have been less active musically, although Harrison had a successful album in 1981, *Somewhere in England*.

The life stories of the Beatles are fascinating, but even more fascinating is the fact that from these rather simple people came something terribly complex. None of them were superb technicians, although Harrison was probably the best player. McCartney has a beautiful voice, but none were startlingly good singers, Starr seldom sang at all, for perhaps good reasons. They developed interesting lyrics, and much has been said about the deep significance of the words in their music. However, for sheer technical reasons, there is little to suggest such phenomenal success. Certainly the presence of George Martin as producer and orchestrator was important, as they came up with one technical innovation after another. The marketing techniques were abundantly successful and the timing was right.

All the standard reasons are appropriate for explaining their success at the beginning. They were an unusual group at that time. However, like all great artists, they had to have something substantive for their success to continue. They were the first to be internationally famous *as a musical group*, as opposed to having one big star. The Beach Boys was another group famous in that era, but even it was identified with Brian Wilson in the early years. The Beatles had no leader; they were all important.

MUSICAL STYLE

For our purposes, all the music before 1962 should be considered pre-Beatles. Although we will discuss that music, it is really not terribly important, nor frankly was it very good. The Beatles can be explained musically in three fairly definitive periods: early Beatles, 1962 to 1964; middle Beatles, 1965 to 1966; and late Beatles, 1967 to 1969. There are not many rock groups that can be so easily classified. This developmental quality makes the Beatles slightly more interesting than other groups. Also, their stylistic periods reflect changes in the times; and although they were a British group, they do reflect changes in American attitudes.

Pre-Beatles

This period begins in 1956 with Lennon and the Quarrymen and extends through the first part of 1962, by which time the Beatles had achieved national prominence in England. This period can be defined as experimental, which is why we will not consider it part of their true musical style.

In 1956, they were little more than a teenage gang, which occasionally beat on musical instruments instead of old ladies. They were heavily influenced by skiffle and were not capable of playing any different kinds of music. At the time Harrison joined the group in 1958, they probably had not progressed much and were essentially three guitarists who had fun making music. They were influenced by a number of musicians, but they were doing very poor imitations. By 1959 they began to pick up momentum, especially with Pete Best as their drummer and the Cavern as a place to play. However, they were still just another group trying to establish a style.

From a musical perspective, the most important event for the Beatles was their experience in Hamburg, Germany, where they were put into competition with other European pop bands. The pop circuit in Europe is somewhat different than in the United States. The demands on musical groups are more diverse, in that they need to play different styles in order to succeed. Also, Hamburg was different from Liverpool, if for no other reason than having a multilingual audience that was used to very loud, almost decadent types of music; the Beatles had to become stronger stage personalities in order to compete. Although there had been some demand for shouting songs in their formative years, by the time they reached Hamburg they had to develop a style which included loud rock and roll.

When they returned to England in 1962, after several trips to Germany, they were seasoned veterans (if not by age, by experience) and had developed a style. With the help of their manager and public relations, they came back to England as successes, and musically they were prepared to deliver.

Early Beatles

Early Beatles music had the following basic stylistic traits:

1. simple lyrics
2. simple background accompaniment
3. rock sound from the 1950s
4. simple drumbeat and rhythmic patterns
5. simple bass lines
6. domination by lead singer or unison singing

The lyrics were basically rock lyrics from the 1950s with relatively little creativity[2]. The songs were primarily about boy-girl relationships on a platonic or nonphysical level. There were a few hard rock tunes, like "A Hard Days Night," but most of them were soft rock in medium tempo. Typical of rock music in the 1950s, the songs were fairly short, roughly the two- to three-minute attention span of young teenagers at that time.

The background accompaniment was well done but simple. However, because it was a little different from that heard in the United States, many people thought the Beatles were strange. The background had a continuous quality with even accents on all four beats. It was skiffle, basically just rhythmic changes with a few chord changes. Interestingly, most of the Beatles' hits were not rhythm and blues; at least they did not use the blues

---

[2]We are overgeneralizing in this section on the Beatles, implying that their early music was simple. In comparison to the times, they did quite a number of things that were highly experimental — they used blues variants and blues singing style in songs which did not use the blues progression; they included unusual instruments; and they used changing accent patterns. However, by comparison to their later music, the music of the pre-Beatles and early Beatles periods was simple.

progression. In all the music in the early period, there were continuous guitar chords, a simple bass line (McCartney was really learning to play the bass and left-handed at that), and continuous four-beat drumming. Ringo's drumming style was pop and did not have the heaviness of rock drummers in the United States.

The Beatles, influenced by Presley, Little Richard, and many others, consciously copied particular traits and songs of other musicians, although they played these tunes with their own style. They used background vocals, mainly screams and woos, and they extensively sang in unison. When there was a lead singer, the other singers provided backgrounds and unison singing for support of the main line.

The rhythmic patterns were also fairly simple, with relatively little riff orientation. The Beatles did not use rhythmic figures to hold a song together but rather relied on the melody. In the early era, at least, they did not develop internal energy through musical devices but rather through stage presence and the "Beatles look."

The bass patterns were pop-oriented and rather simple. Although McCartney would eventually become a competent bass player, his orientation was really toward singing and melody. This interest did not seem to transfer to his bass playing, where he relied mainly on the primary or tonic note of the chord. However, there probably was a lack of models at that time, as the bass line concept had not been developed in rock and roll in the late 1950s.

The lead singer was all-important in early Beatles music, and the two main lead singers, McCartney and Lennon, developed different singing personalities. McCartney was the lyrical and beautiful singer; Lennon was more of a shouter and a strong singer.

One last important thing about the early music is that the Beatles played songs which had little relationship to each other, except that many of them said the same thing. In their albums of this period, the songs were each separate, and there was no real logic to the combinations. In later eras, they would begin to make statements with their selections; in the early era they just sang songs. Fortunately, they were successful and nice songs.

Middle Beatles

The basic stylistic characteristics of middle Beatles were the following:

1. poetically more complex lyrics
2. symbolic lyrics
3. more creative music
4. universal point of view
5. sometimes critical words
6. more guitar-oriented and less percussive
7. folklike
8. more complicated guitar sounds and electronics
9. more subjects in musical lyrics
10. better background accompaniment

The Beatles *(Courtesy of Capitol Records)*

The Beatles really came into their own during the middle period, which began after their fame in the United States. It is hard to imagine that a group could come so far in two or three years, but it must be understood that it was a worldwide group just three years after it had reached some prominence in its own city. By 1965, the Beatles were already wealthy and had at their disposal a number of support mechanisms which rock groups had not previously used. Electronics, technology, and studio techniques were advancing at a very rapid rate in the mid-1960s, and the Beatles had the resources to tap into them. Thus they could make rapid changes, and they did so. This was a period of experimentation for them, but they were experimenting from the top, and that makes a difference.

The first three style characteristics can be illustrated by any song from this era, for example, "Help," "Day Tripper," or "Nowhere Man." The poetry was more complex, and specific words acted as symbols for larger ideas — a basic definition of good poetry. The music was more creative in this period because it did not rely on proven models but rather used new textures. Also, it was aimed at an older audience; it was no longer preteen music.

The music began to take on a universal perspective; that is, it aimed at the world rather than just England or America. Most important was the tendency for the lyrics to be occasionally critical of some institution or segment of society. "Taxman" by George Harrison is a good example of that development, predating the Reagan administration by some years. From careful listening we could discover many nasty slurs about various topics, which illustrates the point that the Beatles saw themselves as commentators on the human condition, and that their music began to contain true messages.

The Beatles' last English tour was in December 1965, and their last British concert was in May 1966. Their last tour in America was in August 1966, which turned out to be their last public appearance. The reasons for the cessation of public activity are related to their reasons for breaking up the group three years later: (1) They were doing the same act over and over, which became boring. (2) They were incapable of using as many effects and extra instruments as they wanted. (3) Performing was becoming dangerous. (4) Generally, touring was unpleasant. (5) Although touring was financially lucrative, it was not as lucrative as other activities. (6) They were beginning to have personality conflicts (although they have not admitted it).

Right after they stopped touring, the group began to splinter. Harrison went with his wife to India. He studied the sitar, a north Indian string instrument, which he used in subsequent Beatles records. John Lennon took a part in the film "How I Won the War." Paul McCartney went to Africa, and Ringo Starr stayed home. Harrison and Lennon were most dedicated to their individual roles, and McCartney was probably the most discontented with the idea of individual Beatles. However, their different activities in the last part of 1966 led to one of their greatest times of creativity, in which drugs, mysticism, and great messages would become most significant.

The music was more guitar-oriented and less percussive, primarily because the songs were more complex and the words more important. The music was folklike, often with three-quarter tempos and very pretty melodies. We do not often associate rock with beautiful folk melodies. Because the message of the song was often associated with the emotions of the words, the Beatles were much more interested in the overall texture of the sound. This development called for less continuous background and a change from the earlier sound of skiffle.

Generally the technical level of the music in the middle era was substantially more complex. Although the Beatles were satisfied with very simple chord constructions in the early style, by the middle period they were sophisticated in the use of rather complex chord progression. Both Harrison and McCartney had become accomplished on their instruments, especially Harrison, and as a result, both the lead guitar and the bass lines improved. With the technical advances available, they became important parts of the texture. Previously the background sound was continuous, without contrast and significance.

That the Beatles considered more subjects in their songs can be confirmed by simply looking at some of the titles. Also the albums of this era began to show some continuity. There was a logic, albeit a loose one, in the way the songs were placed on the albums, and there was consistency in the kinds of sounds. The continued influence of Brian Epstein and George Martin could be heard in the use of larger musical forces in the background.

Late Beatles

The characteristics of the late music were the following:

1. electronic music
2. studio music
3. technically perfect music
4. mystical allusions
5. total communication

The music of the Beatles from 1967 to 1969 was, paradoxically, both diverse and homogeneous. There were traits of the two earlier periods in the music, but the new characteristics made the music more convincing than in any other period. The albums were technical masterpieces, and they may have been artistic masterpieces as well. During this time, there was always an aura of mystery surrounding the Beatles, and this may have been the most important quality of the music of their most mature period.

The four main albums of this era were *Sgt. Pepper's, Magical Mystery Tour, The Beatles* (White Album), and *Abbey Road*.[3] Of course there were others, and perhaps they were more important, but these four albums sum up the group's musical message. Each album was based on the idea of traveling through the world, as a group, on a ship, or simply walking down the street. The Beatles were world travelers, commenting on the world as they journeyed. This image of the traveling musician is an old one and is important in understanding music; in some senses, musicians travel through life and occasionally make valid statements about it.

The Beatles used the most sophisticated studio techniques available to produce their albums. They used many electronic devices to amplify and modify their own sound, and they employed many extra musicians (even the London Symphony Orchestra) to expand the musical texture when it was appropriate. The music could not have been produced in a live performance

---

[3] We did not include *Yellow Submarine* as a major album because it was not exclusively a Beatles' creation.

A Beatles collage *(Courtesy of Capitol Records)*

because of the forces and electronic taping devices required. No matter how far technology goes, especially in microcircuits and miniaturization, rock groups will never be able to perform all their music live; some groups will have to rely on studio performances in order to achieve certain effects (see Chapter Ten).

The Beatles had control of every parameter of music. Whereas they may have been able to crank out an album in a short time during the first part of their career, albums on the scale of the late period took countless hours in performance and then an equal amount of time in redubbing and editing. These were large-scale efforts in comparison to earlier records.

The message of each album was a mystical one, a message given by a group of people who saw themselves as significant commentators on the world, and who felt they were in a position to have influence. "Yellow Submarine," the song and the symbol, can be viewed in many different ways, which is, of course, the mark of truly great poetry or literature. It can be seen as a simple story, without much meaning, or as the story of four people who are out to save the world, protecting it from the loss of true values (that is, music). The albums were commenting on various topics, criticizing, suggesting changes, and pointing out things which might not be obvious but should have been. Allusions to drugs were overt, but they were also part of the message. Although the Beatles did not communicate in the same way as the San Francisco groups, their message was the same. And even though many critics condemned them for it, they were successful in this communication.

However, the most significant part of the late music is that each album, and perhaps the whole period, was organically tied together by a thematic logic. On a particular album, the songs lead one to another, rather than being separate entities. The Beatles finally achieved total communication, in that we must listen to the whole album in order to understand the message. This is a level of sophistication seldom reached by rock groups, or for that matter, by any artist.

Whereas the musical style of the early period was just background sound for the singing, in the late period the musical style was interwoven with the message of the singing. As the orchestra increased in size, so did its complexity and internal integrity.

SUMMARY

Much could be said of the Beatles' marketing techniques and influence, but these topics are common knowledge. Moreover, the marketing of the Beatles is still going on, as we could confirm in any record store. Presley was the most imitated musician of the 1950s, the Beatles of the 1960s. We must wonder why an English group could so accurately reflect that tumultuous time, but the chaos in the United States was reflected all over the world. This particular English group just happened to achieve stardom and wealth at a time when its members could take advantage of their achievements and become the minstrels of the world. It is particularly fitting that they retired at the end of the decade rather than trying to continue, as so many American groups did. Obviously, the Beatles did not quit solely for idealistic reasons, but for those of us who were children of the 1960s, it is a nice thought.

CHAPTER EIGHT

California – North and South

In this chapter we will discuss the difference between music from the southern part of California (that is, Los Angeles) and that from the northern part (that is, San Francisco). We see the musical situation in California as a reflection of what happened in other parts of the United States, just as we saw the Beatles as representing British rock. California is a model for the rest of America, a fact particularly true in the 1960s. It is relatively isolated from the rest of the United States, and there is still a sense of separation from the East.

SOUTHERN CALIFORNIA

In the 1960s, California still represented for many Americans a kind of perfection — in the weather, the beach, and the sunshine. In many ways, southern California lived up to its utopian image. Life was relaxed, the weather was beautiful, and money did not seem to be a problem. There were movie stars, Disneyland, and fast-food stands. Social change could be ignored because life was perfect already.

California was being populated by people from other parts of America because they wanted to share the dream, and southern California was where they wanted to live. Once people became southern Californians, they wanted desperately to keep it to themselves. Even though it was hard to find people who were born there, no one wanted to change the social order. Therefore, it was reasonable that it would be politically conservative. It was also morally conservative. Southern Californians were restrained, although they were outwardly very friendly. The "laid-back" approach is a southern California trait, but it is a relaxed conservative approach rather than the liberal "hang-loose" approach of northern California.

Materialism was very important to people in that area. Cars were necessary both for transportation and for status. In the 1960s the lifestyle in California was hedonistic, and the economic situation supported that philosophy. Success stories were all around, and everyone naturally gravitated toward those patterns of existence.

The lives of youths, at least in the coastal areas, were dominated by visions of the beach or of "hanging out." They could obtain any activity they wanted by driving to it. They could ski in the mountains without having to live with snow, and they could surf in the ocean without having to live with sand. Since they were used to driving short distances (sixty to one hundred miles is considered a short trip in California), they were able to take advantage of the natural resources. And because they were not too concerned with the future, they did not seem to care if those natural resources might not be there in twenty years.

Surfing Music

Pop music in California was really quite diverse. Many of the older generation liked big-band music, which was sometimes associated with the film industry, and there were also many country and western fans. The rock and roll that was popular in the 1950s was the ballad or later styles. California really did not have its own kind of music until surfing music came along. Until that time, the people enjoyed a mixture of pop styles from other parts of the United States.

The Beach Boys *(Courtesy of Capitol Records)*

People normally assume that the kinds of cultural forms which came from California before the 1960s were in fact California-based, but nothing could be further from the truth. The film industry was important to the California lifestyle, as was the entertainment circuit, and there was clearly some association with California tastes. However, entertainers moved to California because the lifestyle was enjoyable and they could get work in a rich industry. But that industry was based on making films and entertainment packages for the rest of the United States. Although they naturally capitalized on the natural resources of California (and those images came through the products), these packages were designed with the viewer in Des Moines or upstate New York in mind.

Surfing music was a result of a growing population of young people in southern California, a population which had significant wealth. At first, the music was primarily designed for large dances held in public places on the ocean. Then it became packaged and sold much as Presley had been sold. There were more surfing bands than could be imagined, and they had a proven model. The originator of the form was Brian Wilson, who founded the Beach Boys. The model he generated was truly unique, and in the intense desire to share in that success, most of the other surf bands turned out song after song that sounded exactly like the original. In short, surfing music was unique, but once we had heard one surfing song we knew all the musical characteristics of the style. Everything else sounded the same.

The story of the Beach Boys would not be so interesting if they had not eventually progressed beyond that original model, which of course they did. But the point is that they invented something pretty clever, and the basic model worked very well, was extremely popular, and still has validity today. Surfing music reflects attitudes in southern California, and thus is a perfect model for art reflecting life.

The Beach Boys represented the image of the southern Californian. They all lived in Hawthorne, were clean cut, went to school, and surfed after school (well, maybe not Wilson). Wilson was musically creative and formed a group with his two brothers — Carl on guitar and Dennis on drums. The original group also had as members Mike Love and Al Jardine. By 1962, Wilson had formed the group around the idea that it would sing surfing songs in a mostly vocal style, with a background that was smooth and continuous. The music was different from that of the Beatles in their formative years, maybe not much better but much smoother. The vocal patterns were mostly sung in unison, but they did contain some harmony. Wilson sang in a falsetto voice, and the group in harmony sometimes sounded like the Hi-Lo's or the Four Freshmen. The combination of surfing songs and the sound of the Beach Boys was unique at the time, and Wilson had the energy to keep doing it the same way until he got it right.

In 1963, he adapted "Sweet Little Sixteen" by Chuck Berry and turned it into "Surfin' U.S.A.," which helped the group achieve national fame. Surfing music was really designed for southern California, but it also worked in places where surf had never been seen. The Beach Boys were popular in California, but eventually they became even more popular in the Midwest and in other places in America. Wilson wrote a number of surfing songs during the first few years of the group's existence, and he also wrote for Jan and Dean, who rode the model to success.

The music of the Beach Boys can be conveniently broken up into two stylistic periods, although some critics may be tempted to add a third period

The Beach Boys in concert, 1980 *(Photo by Barry Rankin)*

for material from the late 1970s. We will consider two periods — one before and one after 1966. The first period can be defined in terms of the kinds of topics about which they sang, basically the following:

1. girls
2. cars
3. surf, sun, and beach
4. devotion

The "girl" songs are brilliantly uncluttered with real emotion, in that they exist on a platonic level. They depict removed love and are simple in context. The lyrics express ideas of protectiveness ("Don't Hurt My Little Sister") and puppy love. They are simple, but they are very touching.

Some of the best songs from the first period are the "car" songs (or "cartunes" if you wish). These are simple models for materialism and identification with the power technology of southern California. Many teenagers spent hours after school riding around in "cool" cars, and these songs pay homage to that fact. "Little Deuce Coupe" or "409" are great songs, if only for the simplicity of the message. "Little Old Lady from Pasadena" is probably one of the cleverest novelty tunes from the history of the art form. The car became a person in these songs, a person with whom we could entrust major parts of our ego. To think that these songs do not invoke valid nostalgic emotion today is to ignore a part of our reality.

The "surf" songs are classics and pivotal to the image of the Beach Boys. Songs like "Warmth of the Sun" are real in southern California and can be especially pleasing to someone in the upper Midwest during the last part of winter. These songs evoke feelings of a simple life in which we need not worry about double-digit inflation or war. Part of the appeal of this first period is that the types of songs allowed us to forget about reality.

"Devotion" songs usually had something to do with a particular institution and the good things in it. For example, in "Be True to Your School," the Beach Boys invoke the all-American image of our school being the best around. That value is sadly gone today, but the songs of the early Beach Boys can bring it back, if only for a minute.

Musically, the first period is pretty easy to define: continuous singing with uncomplicated harmony, rhythm, and backgrounds. If we listen carefully, we can hear cheerleading kinds of things in the background figures, like rah-rah-rah, sis-boom-bah or other nonsense words. The Beatles also used simple phrases like these; simplicity often works best.

In the second half of 1966, Brian Wilson stopped touring with the group and was replaced by Bruce Johnston (his song, "Disney Girls," was on the *Surf's Up* album of 1971). Wilson had a good marketing technique for the Beach Boys and was brilliant in creating the model. However, for a variety of personal reasons, he stopped having a direct impact on the group in terms of growth, and Carl Wilson, who had been the silent partner up to this point, took over. The Beach Boys began to lose their clean-cut image, growing longer hair and beards, and they began to experiment (especially with electronics) and to make social comment.

Brian Wilson went into collaboration with Van Dyke Parks, a poet and lyricist, with whom he created songs in a new image. This association was to continue for years, although Wilson returned to the Beach Boys on a sporadic basis. His songs created with Parks have been poetically more complex and socially significant and a great deal more contemporary. Probably the most significant album in the collaboration is *Pet Sounds*, made in 1967. It contains experimentation equal to that of the Beatles, especially in its complex melodies and dense harmonies. The poetry is quite complicated in comparison to early Beach Boys material. Several songs in collaboration with Parks appear on the *Surf's Up* album.

The process of change to this 1971 album was slow. The Beach Boys continued to tour between 1966 and 1971 and to sing songs of the first era. But by 1971, when they produced *Surf's Up*, they had changed almost completely. They began to reflect societal views, and they were critical in songs like "Student Demonstration Time." This album, which also contains songs about the ecology, has more complicated lyrics in comparison to earlier material. Their sound was different, and although they still could sing and play in a

Brian Wilson of the Beach Boys, taken in 1980 *(Photo by Barry Rankin)*

smooth style, they often did not. "Student Demonstration Time" sounds an awful lot like Bob Dylan, someone whom they certainly would not have imitated in a song about cars or surfing. Even the title song does not sound at all like an early tune. In this album, the Beach Boys are asking serious questions, something a southern Californian simply did not do in the early 1960s. In essence, the influences of San Francisco had been felt, even by the Beach Boys.

Nonsurfing Music

There was an underground movement in southern California which eventually produced some significant musicians (see Chapter Twelve). Probably the most significant group in Los Angeles that was not surf-oriented was Jim Morrison and the Doors. Morrison was an extremely high-energy rock singer who teamed up with Ray Manzarek, a rhythm and blues piano player originally from Chicago. Although a blues-based band (somewhat like the Rolling Stones), it established itself as a national success in 1967 with its first album, *The Doors*. These musicians were ahead of their time in Los Angeles but not in the rest of America. Their main lyrical themes were sex and death in a very blatant style. In their theatricality, they were almost pre-punk. They were very important until Morrison's death in 1971.

NORTHERN CALIFORNIA

The difference in attitudes between Los Angeles and San Francisco is striking. First, the climates are totally different. San Francisco is another waterfront town, but it has a grand harbor with hills and fog. It rains a lot and the weather is colder, not like the Midwest, but damp cold. It is, relatively speaking, a much more sophisticated town. Where Los Angeles is a relaxed community of sun worshippers, San Francisco is artistic, cultured, and just a bit snobbish. It is historically significant, being associated with the gold rush and migration from the East. It was the port for immigrants from the Orient and was involved in the building of the railroad. Its history is no longer than that of Los Angeles, but it is substantially more cosmopolitan. Although both towns have Spanish names, La Ciudad de Los Angeles is much more Spanish-American in culture.

While southern California had quick increases in population, San Francisco stayed basically the same. The people there did not take to the surfing tradition at all, and it was not until the mid-1960s that the city began to develop its own musical tradition. But the San Francisco sound was to become more important to the history of rock than surfing music, not in record sales or money, but in influence.

As the bastion of liberalism, specifically at the University of California, Berkeley, San Francisco became a hotbed for new and radical ideas. The first significant movement was the free-speech movement, which probably started as early as 1963. The first music associated with it was folk music, which became the focus for the rock music which eventually sprang from it. The folk music of San Francisco was radical; that is, it carried an intrinsic message that parts of society had to change — "The Times They Are a - Changin'."

The student movement carried with it a number of ideas which brought youth and oppressed people together. From it evolved the hippie movement, with its central concepts of love and freedom, the vehicle being drugs. Sexual freedom and freedom of lifestyle created communal living in places like Haight-Ashbury, a section of San Francisco. Although there were communities of hippies living elsewhere in the United States (for example, in Venice, near Los Angeles), the hippie community in San Francisco was stronger because of its association with Berkeley. For many reasons (its liberalness being the major one) San Francisco developed itself as the center of the movement, and musically, folk music turned into a particular kind of rock.

Acid Rock

The San Francisco sound can be labeled *acid rock* or *psychedelic rock*, which means that it is associated with LSD, or acid. Although this is a debatable issue, the kind of music people listen to while taking acid probably needs to be loud, or at least the chroniclers of this kind of music suggest that it should be loud. It is simple music because, frankly, it is difficult to discriminate different sounds at high-volume levels. The lead guitar plays a very important role in acid rock, as do lights and other special effects. Acid rock is the kind of music which is said to cause hearing loss.

San Francisco rock became associated with very loud music and a deafening use of electronic amplification. It has had an influence on many other rock musicians and led to increased use of electronics and multiple banks of speakers. In the late 1960s, it was responsible for more than one complete electrical failure in theaters where these kinds of bands were booked. The function of acid rock is to provide a stimulus for the total experience of the people involved, musicians and audience alike. It is not like a concert in which people sit in straight rows, separate from the performers. The entire crowd and the band become part of the musical and physical experience. The music is meant to be felt rather than just heard, and anyone who has ever attended a performance of an acid group knows that it can be felt. Amplifiers are turned up to the breaking point, and there is a great deal of created distortion.

Although acid rock could be understood as an extension of the shouting tradition from the 1950s, it is really much more intense. The emphasis is on loud sounds from the lead guitar and the singer, although the words themselves are not very significant. The singer functions as another part of the musical texture, and it is very hard to distinguish the words. Acid rock could not succeed on the power of the words (that is, their meaning) alone. It is the total art work that is important, not any one part.

The subject matter of acid rock is normally antiestablishment and/or drug-oriented. San Francisco rock was designed for a particular audience in a particular state of mind; therefore, it was not designed for mass consumption, which it seldom achieved. It was quite clearly a cult type of music, although it would eventually have somewhat wider implications. Other than folk rock it was the message of the 1960s, much more so than the music of the Beach Boys.

To understand its musical and technical characteristics, it is probably necessary to listen to acid rock under certain controlled situations. (*We are not recommending drugs!*) We need powerful amplifiers and speakers so that the volume can be turned up. Acid rock is not successful at low volumes because the experience was not meant to be soft. Therefore, if we want to experience the music as it was intended, we have to turn up the volume. The same thing can be said about some groups from the 1970s, the Who, for example.

In the following section, we will discuss four groups from San Francisco who exemplified this kind of music: Moby Grape, Jefferson Airplane, Big Brother and the Holding Company, and the Grateful Dead. All these groups were most significant in the 1960s, even though some of their musicians are still around; the Grateful Dead still performs together, although its musicians seem a little older and a little tamer. As usual, there are other groups we could have chosen, but these are good representatives.

Acid Groups

Moby Grape lasted for about two years, after which the members broke up and joined other groups or worked as singles. However, from May 1967 to 1969, Moby Grape was a fairly important group, combining country, folk, pop, and rock with psychedelic elements. Its music was quite strong and its act was definitely psychedelic. Probably its most interesting album was released in April 1968, a two-record set called *Wow/Grape Jams, Grape Jams* featured spontaneous improvisation by several guest artists — Al Kooper, the organist from Blood, Sweat and Tears, and Mike Bloomfield, guitarist with Electric Flag. These jams, or free improvisations, illustrate the basic style of acid rock in the spontaneous energy of the melodic runs. It is very powerful music and is done rather cleverly. In some sense, Moby Grape was a fairly soft version of acid rock, but it had all the elements of a psychedelic band.

Jefferson Airplane was an important and lasting group. It began in 1966 and was the most influential of the San Francisco bands, probably because of Grace Slick, who was a powerful and attractive singer. The message of the Airplane was drugs, and many of the songs were strictly about drugs. The band used a psychedelic advertising package and was the first San Francisco group to be successful in New York. It had an amazing potpourri of musical styles — blues, folk, jazz, rock — and in San Francisco-type crowds, was very free in performances. The members exhibited that quality of "hanging loose," but they were very controlled within their freedom. They made extensive use of light shows and were the first to work out the light show so that it completely supported the music.

The Airplane was of course analogous to the Beatles in the *Yellow Submarine*. Its members were traveling in this symbolic manner to bring their message to the world, and their theme song, "Fly Jefferson Airplane," became the chief message. In songs like "White Rabbit" they told us what life was about and incidentally reminded us of what *Alice in Wonderland* was really implying. Other people had known about the drug allusion in Lewis Carroll's tale, but the Jefferson Airplane advertised the idea. Besides the packaging, Jefferson Airplane was a competent group of musicians, and Grace Slick's voice was significant in terms of its impact. In the mid-1970s, it changed its name to Jefferson Starship and continued to enjoy some success.

Big Brother and the Holding Company was a group of the late 1960s, the peak of their popularity being in 1968. The strength of this group was in its musicality as it supported the enormous talent of Janis Joplin. Although Grace Slick was the first female singer to be highly successful with a rock band (at least in the white tradition), Joplin was probably more important. At the Monterey Festival in 1967, she brought the house down because she was so

Jefferson Airplane *(Courtesy of RCA Records)*

strong, sexual, and different. Her singing style was straight from the rhythm and blues tradition, and in fact, before joining Big Brother, she was a powerhouse blues singer (even though she was quite young). Her singing style was gutsy. She used groans and all the old blues tricks, and her voice was raspy and almost masculine.

Although not an extremely beautiful woman, Joplin had an erotic way about her and absolutely captivated audiences. She exhibited the same power that Jimi Hendrix did with his guitar. Like Little Richard a decade earlier, Joplin made you feel the pain she was going through, and she used every part of her body to communicate it. She was undoubtedly the most powerful female performer of the rock era and has continued to serve as a model for other women in rock and roll — Blondie, for instance.

The Grateful Dead is the supreme acid band, and it functioned as the leader of the cult. It was idealized in Tom Wolfe's *The Electric Kool-Aid Acid Test* as the group that traveled around and spread the message, that is, LSD. The image in that book was that of a bus painted with psychedelic messages and a huge stereo system traveling around America, giving away acid and

Jefferson Airplane *(Courtesy of RCA Records)*

putting it into water reservoirs. The statement is constantly made, "You're either on the bus or you're off the bus."

The lead guitar player, Jerry Garcia, has been the molding force of the Dead, which originally began as a country and blues band. It started in 1966 and was most popular between 1967 and 1969. However, unlike some of the bands in this era, it is still performing in basically the same style today. Surprisingly, the Grateful Dead is not loud or shocking. It became the center of attention because of its commitment to the San Francisco movement and only incidentally because of its music. The members lived in Haight-Ashbury and were a part of the "love-in" and "flower child" attitude. They lived like members of the commune and played for countless hippie parties. They have given more free concerts than any other big-name band and have endeared themselves to the community that immortalized them. The Grateful Dead became the symbol for the San Francisco sound and for its music because its members were a true part of the movement.

Their music is psychedelic, but in a kind of relaxed way. Although they may have seemed shocking at the time, there were other bands who took what they did much further, Black Sabbath, for instance, or later, Kiss. But the Grateful Dead were and still are solid rock and blues musicians, and their songs were powerful within the context of the times. The fact that they are still around speaks to the universality and competency of their music.

SUMMARY

The psychedelic bands were important to the development of rock for several reasons. Rock had after all lost its identification as a movement, and the acid bands united that identification with rebellion. The San Francisco sound, which combined folk music with rock, became the central symbol for the student rights movement, the sexual revolution, the drug revolution, and ultimately the antiwar movement. It was a way by which youth could stand apart from the older generation, and the history of rock gains momentum every time a way is found to rebel against the establishment.

Acid rock was significant in that it represented a time of great freedom for youth and, at first, a significant change in philosophy. Young people wanted to be free of the restrictions of contemporary society. They sought a release and an escape. Unfortunately, as the drug movement became more and more dangerous because of decadent intervention, and the flower child society began to break down, acid rock started to lose its significance, even though its influence would continue into the 1970s. This was not an affluent movement, and it did not make a lot of money. However, that is precisely what the San Francisco movement was all about, that is, rejecting the materialism of the 1950s. In some ways, acid rock was a reaction against what was successful in southern California in the early and mid-1960s; it was San Francisco's response to Los Angeles. The interesting thing is that the San Francisco sound was eventually influential on the leader of southern California music, the Beach Boys.

CHAPTER NINE

Attitudes of the 1970s

As we get closer to the present, it becomes harder to generalize about attitudes. Whereas the 1960s are really history, the 1970s are almost the present. Although it is hard to tell when attitudes shifted and when they ended, it is easy to identify the 1960s as a time of social change and to describe the various movements. Probably the best way to deal with the 1970s is to say that its attitudes were those which ran counter to the movements of the previous decade, although some attitudes of the 1960s may have reemerged during the 1970s and early 1980s.

The election of Richard Nixon in 1968 was certainly a signal for the end of the decade. Of course, his election was partially a result of the typical reaction against the status quo, but in this case it also represented a shift backward in time. People wanted to return to a hard-line approach toward communism, and probably the more important point, they also wanted a controlled society.

The 1960s reflected constant change, which was confusing to people, even to those who were not changing themselves. The Vietnam War had a devastating effect on America, perhaps more so than was realized. It was, after all, a war which was undeclared and which America did not seem to be winning. We entered it as an advisor and found ourselves drawn into the actual fighting. In previous wars, we were clearly on one side, a side which was being oppressed according to our point of view. In South Vietnam, the enemy was nebulous.

The election of Nixon represented frustration with the uncontrollable state of the 1960s, in a sense a desire for solidarity. His election reflected a wish on the part of middle America for a return to the old days, even though that was of course not possible.

Even Nixon must have realized that the attitudes of the 1950s were no longer relevant, but this did not stop him from implying that they were, especially in his second campaign for the presidency in 1968. After being elected, he moved very quickly to establish a position of strength. He offered a real alternative to the confusion of the 1960s and ushered in a new era of conservative control.

Another important event in the early 1970s was the Watergate scandal, which affected the public on the same level psychologically as the Vietnam War. The Vietnam conflict had ended and we lost face as a result of it. However, Watergate was to drop a great blanket on our trust in government. Everything ugly in American society was reflected in Watergate, which was devastating in its impact. Society had changed, and the result was massive depression. The American people had lost faith in our government; it does not seem as if we got it back during the 1970s.

Jimmy Carter was elected in 1976 as an outsider in Washington. His promise was to manage the government and to remove the stigma of power politics. Whether or not he succeeded will be judged by history, but he was not successful in maintaining a positive image over time. It is probably accurate that Carter failed in his reelection bid because of the times rather than any innate weakness in himself or his programs. Some have predicted that no American president will ever again serve more than one term and that they will all be considered failures.

Although the United States has always seemed to be concerned about the rest of the world, it is the author's opinion that our significance shifted in the 1970s from its previous position of strength. We were no longer the undisputed leader of the world, and some of the events of the 1970s reinforced that idea. Our involvement in world politics (both in Vietnam and in the Middle East) was not as successful as we had expected. The influence of Vietnam was crushing, but the experience in Iran was even worse, although less costly in human life. We were completely defeated in Iran, and the world watched us as we were powerless.

The 1970s also witnessed an increase in communism, especially in Europe. This has changed our negotiating position in the world, and the threat of communism is no longer as simple as it was perceived in the 1950s. One cannot simply hate Russia or China (especially since a conservative President Nixon opened the way for communication and was applauded for it), because communism is currently accepted throughout the world. It is simply another alternative, and like rock and roll it will not go away.

The election of Ronald Reagan and the Prime Ministership of Margaret Thatcher are obvious signals that people would like to regain control. Reagan was certainly elected out of the same desire of the people as was Carter, that is, that this man will control the government and make it as it was in the past. While it is debatable whether he has succeeded, the important point is that he symbolizes a desire for a return to the past, those glory years when America was number one.

The economic climate of the 1970s and early 1980s is substantially different from the previous two decades. Some have said that 1982, for instance, was the worst economic year since the great depression of 1929. The difference is that there may be little that we can do about current depressions, and that in itself is reason for depression. The 1970s in general saw one financial crisis after another, with double-digit inflation, rising unemployment, and cutback after cutback in social programs. Trust levels went way down as a result of these economic pressures, and the previous concern for the good of all the people seemed to ebb quite quickly.

We were pressed by many problems both within and without the United States — the oil crisis (both here and abroad), inflation in general, increased complexity, corruption within the various social programs and social security, international terrorism and political blackmail, and the conflict between taking care of our own people and helping others and especially our own government. As we were pushed harder and harder, our reaction against government and other controllers became stronger, ultimately leading to the election of Reagan, who promised to defeat the bureaucratic dragon.

The 1970s saw a return to materialism. They also became a time in which the main concern was protecting ourselves rather than fighting for the protection of others. The political climate was such that Americans began to defend themselves against outsiders.

The idealism of the 1960s died for another reason: The movements had been as successful as they could have been, and they had begun to breed corruption from within. One example will indicate the general state. At Kent State in 1970, the National Guard was brought in to control a riot, and four students were killed. We will not make value judgments about the legality or morality of that particular action, but it does reflect a changing concept toward demonstrations. From that point on, any changes in society would have to be accomplished through regular processes. As the movements died of their own impetus, routine process took over. Therefore, we see the 1970s as the time of the great bureaucrat.

Many of the previously mentioned events of the 1970s led to a shift in psychological attitude, influencing everything in society, including morality.

One of the major influences was the technological explosion, which began in the late 1950s. During the 1970s, we witnessed an expansion of technical capability previously unmatched by any other era in history. Communications in particular became much more sophisticated, and information was available instantaneously. This alone may have been one of the most significant dehumanizing factors of the 1970s.

Computers were capable of producing immediate readouts on each of us, and they also provided services, such as credit card systems, computerized billing, and video games. While it is certainly debatable whether these developments were good or bad, some of our difficulties can be directly traced to human inability to control or adapt to technology. Many people went under financially because of credit cards, computerized billing can drive you up the wall when there is a mistake, and who can imagine living without Pac Man.

Morality changed considerably in the 1970s; one could assert that it decayed. While many applaud the advances made by minorities and women during the 1970s, there has also been a negative aspect to those advancements. So much concern for the individual has caused a movement away from concern for others and for pure ideals. Most things are thought of in technical terms or in political terms and very seldom in moral or ethical terms.

While not all developments were depressing in the 1970s and early 1980s, it does seem to be a troubled time. The main problem is that nothing can be done to reignite the feelings of the 1950s and 1960s. Technology cannot be controlled; we will probably never again have a stable economy (much less an expanding one); and our place in the world is no longer that of undisputed leader. While we can still be creative and dynamic within our limits, we must recognize those limits in order to achieve any success. Whether or not these political and social judgments are thoroughly correct, society in the 1970s and early 1980s reflected a negativism that seemed to have no positive alternatives.

CHAPTER TEN

Technology and Electronics

Change in electronic technology over the last thirty years has been phenomenal. Scientific change in general has had a major influence on society, both in its viewpoint and in its physical life. Technological change has always had a massive effect on human society. No matter what the technological advancement, there is always a reaction to it, sometimes positive and sometimes negative.

However, since World War II, the world has experienced technological change at a seemingly impossible rate. Although it is certain that other eras felt the change as much as we have, somehow our reaction to it has been stronger, if for no other reason than the speed of change. We have had less time to get used to change before the next advancement is upon us.

Although technology has affected everything in our society, it has been especially important to rock music. Music in general has become an electronic art in the last thirty to forty years, and rock has been a leader in that movement. In this chapter, we will discuss primarily electronic devices. It should be understood that there were nonelectronic devices created during the history of rock and roll which were significant in its ability to proliferate. An example is the invention of high-speed record-producing machines, whereby thousands of records could be produced in one week in order to meet the demand created by the marketing techniques discussed earlier.

For purposes of the following discussion, we will divide our topic as follows: amplifiers, microphones, and sound systems; special effects; synthesizers; and extramusical effects. Although this discussion will not cover all the influences of electronics and/or technology on rock, it will certainly give some idea of the tremendous ramifications of new devices. Finally, we will try to point out the way in which these instruments have helped create the constituent parts of a rock performance. It should be understood that without these electronic advancements, we might still be singing "Rock Around the Clock" (that is, a mechanical one).

AMPLIFIERS, MICROPHONES, AND SOUND SYSTEMS

The state of the art for sound systems in the early 1950s was still fairly primitive. Most of the portable sound systems were bulky and relatively inefficient. It took a tremendous amount of power to drive speakers, and the systems had numerous problems.

The best way to view a sound system is as a three-part process: a microphone to pick up the sound, an amplifier to change the signal into pure electricity and to intensify it, and a speaker to change the electronic signal back into physical sound. This audio chain, like any chain, is only as strong as its weakest link. In the 1950s, almost every part of the chain was fairly weak, with the possible exception of the speakers.

Microphones in the late 1940s and early 1950s were rather cumbersome. The best were large, were made out of materials which broke easily, and did not pick up all the sound. They were adequate in a studio, but in live performances were more apt to produce the sound of a football stadium than high-quality music. They simply did not have the capacity to pick up the spectrum of sound necessary for the performance of diversified textures. Thus, many of the singers of that time sounded awfully thin.

Amplifiers, made up of electronic circuits which used vacuum tubes, also had some structural deficiencies, although frankly the same basic concept is used in highly successful amplifiers on the market today. Their main difficulty was in maintenance and in stamina. They gave out easily and were not capable of sustaining the high power needed for the production of complex and/or loud music. Many musicians who performed in the 1950s can remember the agony of hearing an amplifier begin to self-destruct and the ensuing agony of picking the monster up and getting it fixed. Some of the old bass and guitar amplifiers (which were really the entire audio chain in one cabinet) were notorious for their self-destruct mechanism. They always seemed to break down after the first number and at times caught fire while they were doing it.

Speakers of earlier eras were basically the same as today, although the housing was somewhat more primitive. They tended to break down much more easily because of the way they were fastened to the speaker box. Most of the changes in speakers have been concerned with reshaping the container for increased sensitivity and strength. It was quite common in earlier years to see speakers completely fall apart under high power and even to shoot out through the speaker cabinet, occasionally hitting the musician where it really hurts.

The purpose of the audio chain is to project the sound into the audience, but in a way that is artistically satisfying. Some of the changes which occurred over the years were as follows:

1. use of solid state construction (that is, transistors)
2. improvement of cables to join the various parts
3. addition of preamplifiers to begin the process of changing the sound and allowing for special effects
4. use of graphic equalizers to change the harmonic texture of the sound and to eliminate feedback
5. use of multiple speakers for audience acoustics and monitor speakers on stage for the musicians

Of course, the general change over the years has been miniaturization — putting more power in a smaller space. Technology has continued to advance the electronic capabilities of sound systems, thereby increasing the quality of sound projected and making possible the production of certain effects.

A good sound engineer can change the actual sound of a musical group by simply knowing what to do with a graphic equalizer or a mixing board. It is now quite common for musicians to use as many as twelve different microphones to pick up all the different musical sounds being reproduced. The sound engineer is responsible for providing a pleasing mixture of these sounds, being sensitive to what is happening on a moment-to-moment basis in the performance and being quick enough to tune out any unwanted distortion or feedback. It takes a very good musical ear to hear that at six thousand cycles per second there is feedback.

SPECIAL EFFECTS

Many special effects machines have been created for the musician. Some are particularly oriented toward the rock musician, but they have also been used effectively by jazz, folk, country, and studio musicians. Most of the special effects were first used as studio recording devices, and then they were mass marketed for public performances. No musician can survive without knowing about special effects, and we would hope, using them tastefully.

Some of the first effects used were mechanical, but today most are electronic, derived from the synthesizer. One of the first completely mechanical special effects on the guitar was the Palm Pedal, also called a Tremelo Arm. This was simply a small handle built into the face of the guitar, by which the level of the pitches could be raised by stretching the strings tighter. They are still available today and are used extensively by country musicians. The first musician to use one as a definite part of his style was Duane Eddy.

Electronic effects include the following: Wah-Wah, Fuzz, Phase Shifter, Flanger, Chorus, Harmonizer, and Envelope. These are all pedal devices and can be used with guitar, piano, or any other amplified instrument. They all produce relatively instantaneous changes in the amplified sound coming out of the instrument after it goes through a microphone (the microphone can be connected directly to the instrument).

Electronic microphones can be connected to instruments. Some of the most interesting are the Barcus-Berry units, which can be attached directly to guitars, basses, and pianos. They can also be used for flutes, saxophones, clarinets, trumpets, trombones, and other instruments (including a Japanese Koto).

Although also electronic, a special class of effects is the echo. These effects began as Reverb pedals, which simply caused an instantaneous repetition of whatever was being amplified. A further modification is the Echoplex, which controls the intensity and the time delay of the reverberation. The Echoplex has been effectively used by many musicians, both live and in the studio. Another interesting effect is the Duplicator or Octave Divider, which reproduces electronically and simultaneously an amplification an octave or two octaves below the originally played pitch. This is a most effective device because it really enhances the sound of an instrument like the trumpet or saxophone. With proper use of these effects, we can make one saxophone sound like a whole horn section, or, in other words, we can reproduce Chicago all by ourselves.

SYNTHESIZERS

The synthesizer is certainly the most important musical instrument developed in the twentieth century, with the electric piano a close second. The synthesizer was not developed as a rock instrument, although since its invention in the 1950s it has become an extremely important part of the rock world, most notably in the 1970s.

The synthesizer is simply a machine which reproduces sound, and in that sense it is like a traditional musical instrument. However, the main difference is that it is totally electronic, except for the keyboards and manual switches. A synthesizer is a collection of oscillators (electronic boxes which produce single pitches) tied together with circuitry and controls. It can create any kind of individual sound desired — pitch, duration, intensity, and quality (or timbre) — and allows for multiple reproduction (many sounds at once). The difference between a synthesizer and traditional musical instruments is that depending on the sophistication of the former, the musician can produce virtually anything under the sun — the sound of a trumpet, a violin, and a church organ, or the sound of wind and surf. It is a versatile machine that can be used like a piano or guitar and can be hooked up to special effects.

The history of the synthesizer is rather interesting. It was developed in the 1950s as a way to compose and perform electronic music more quickly. Previously, composers of "new music," as it was called, used either a tape recorder to tape natural sounds (then they glued the pieces of tape together) or banks of oscillators and lots of chords to connect them. Therefore, the first synthesizers were mainly composers' instruments and were not at all suited to live performances. They also played only one note at a time, and they would have needed a Mack truck to carry from one place to another.

Dr. Robert Moog, a physicist, developed the synthesizer, and after some experimentation, he created a smaller unit which was in fact fairly portable. It still created one note at a time, but it could be used in live performance. By the mid-1970s, polyphonic (multivoiced) synthesizers were available; now few rock bands exist without them. They are normally used like a special effect and are placed on top of the electric piano or organ. However, some heavy funk or jazz-rock musicians use them exclusively as part of the rhythmic and melodic ensemble. Also, synthesizer solos are now quite commonplace.

EXTRAMUSICAL EFFECTS

The most obvious extramusical effects are nonelectronic, such as the way that a performer moves and/or dresses. The 1970s became the electronic era on stage as well as in society, and the stage look of rock became increasingly more power-oriented. Some mechanical effects like smoke screens and dummies were used by groups like the Who and the notorious Kiss. However, the more interesting effects were in fact electronic.

Light shows became a very important part of the rock arsenal. At first they were simply multiple spotlight setups. However, by the mid-1970s they were attached to the music so that lights came off and on according to the beat. They also have been rigged so that they could change colors according to either a preset pattern or to the changes in the electronics on stage. They have even been set by minicomputers, responding to the texture of the sound. This development has created a multidimensional art form.

Musicians have also used film and electronically produced crowd noises and/or background sounds. Therefore, electronics have completely dominated not only the sound of the ensemble but also its performance. Electronics have even enhanced the way a rock performance evolves, such as the Dolby effects used in rock films, like *Tommy*, and more recently, *Flash Gordon*.

SUMMARY

Electronic effects were developed because musicians wanted to create distortion that had previously been accomplished by turning the system against itself (either the guitar itself or the microphone was pointed into the speaker which amplified it). Although functional, this system quite often caused uncontrolled noise. Special effects provided control.

However, it should be understood that as the special effects were developed for specific applications, they in turn created the possibilities of other applications. In other words, the electronics which were created in turn created other electronics and further uses of the new equipment. It was a building-block process in which invention was the mother of invention. To view electronics as simple handmaidens of the process is to miss part of their significance. These technological advancements were truly part of the creative process because they allowed things to happen which would not have happened without them.

The electronics of rock have been influential in the development and significance of the art form from a technical point of view, but they have also become its conscious expression. Perhaps no other art form is so totally tied to the scientific explosion of the twentieth century, because no other art form has a history which is so directly contemporary with it. The expansion of electronics and the post-World War II technical world are equivalent to the history of rock; they both happened at the same time.

CHAPTER ELEVEN

English Rock

As the next four chapters sum up the history of rock in the 1970s and early 1980s, it is appropriate to point out here that the chapters are organized according to topics or styles rather than chronology. For some of the topics the discussion will start with developments in the 1960s and end in the 1970s. The style of music in the former decade sometimes led conclusively to its continuation in the latter, and it is better to consider that overall sweep rather than trying to force the style into two periods. Where there are different styles which correspond to the different decades, we will indicate that fact.

Also, it was our contention that music of the 1950s and its extension into the early 1960s was more appropriately named *rock and roll*, and that the music from the mid-Beatles on should be considered *rock*. Our basic position is that this change resulted from rock becoming a way of life (a philosophy affecting clothing, political views, and all other aspects of existence). It was at this point that we began to use the term *rock*. The chart on page *120* illustrates various movements in rock until 1971, and it should indicate the complexity of the art form.

POST-BEATLES BRITISH ROCK

We are of course guilty of seeing rock and roll as a particularly American phenomenon, allowing for the influence of African music through Afro-American tradition. However, it is the purpose of this chapter to outline the significance of British rock bands through three examples. Cited in the Bibliography are materials that provide more complete coverage.

English rock includes a tremendous diversity of styles, and, at least in the post-Beatles stage, it continues to have an effect on American rock and pop music around the world. Rock was a worldwide phenomenon in the 1970s, and the exclusion from this book of rock groups from non-English-speaking countries does not imply that such groups do not exist. For example, probably the most significant and successful European rock group in the 1970s was ABBA, but it did not influence subsequent groups or set new trends.

In this chapter we will discuss the Rolling Stones, who were contemporary with the Beatles but who have remained active up to the present. We will also discuss the Who, which had major impact in the late 1960s and early 1970s, and we will comment on Elton John as one of the most significant rock musicians of the mid-1970s. In Chapter Fourteen we will discuss several British musicians in the late 1970s because Britain was the leader in both punk and new wave music.

English rock has a distinctive sound for several reasons:

1. Depending on their upbringing, the musicians speak and sing with a distinctive accent, and of course they use British English.

2. There is a slight influence of skiffle in the beginning stages of music from the 1960s.

3. The technology of the amplified sound is different, in that the amplifiers are set to amplify the harmonic spectrum differently in Britain than in America.

4. Musical symbolism tends to be different and at times draws from the literary tradition of Europe.

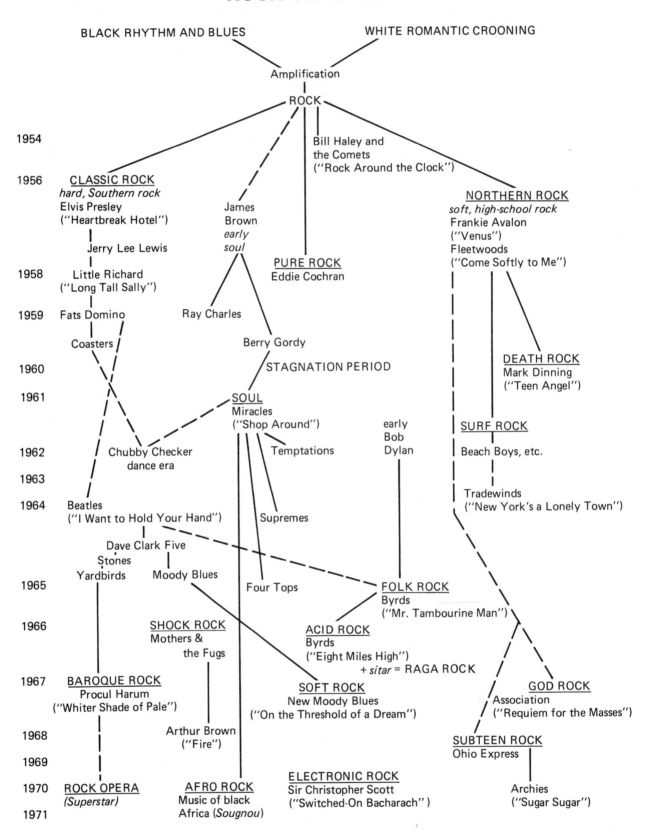

5. The blending of voices tends to be less emotional and at times rougher in quality.

The Rolling Stones

This group began in the early 1960s. There is a great deal of debate about its image and precisely what it represents. Our position is that it ultimately reflects attitudes of the 1970s. If punk rock is an artistic response to the 1970s, then rock bands that reflect punk attitudes in the 1960s are in fact ahead of their time. The Rolling Stones fit any model of punk (as perhaps the Who does also), and therefore, its philosophical image is one of the 1970s.

Mick Jagger, Brian Jones, and Keith Richard were the three original Stones. Jagger and Richard had actually gone to school with each other when they were six years old, but it was in 1960 that they met as musicians. At the age of seventeen, they were both aspiring musicians in rhythm and blues, which at that time was an expanding entertainment form in England. They joined several other musicians, including Charlie Watts on drums, to form a group called the Blues Boys, not to be confused with the Blues Brothers. At this point, they were pretty rough, and their group included several juvenile delinquents. In 1962, they added bass player Bill Wyman, and in 1963 Charlie Watts joined permanently. In 1963, they signed on as one of their managers Andrew Oldham, who was to have significant impact in building their image.

The music of the Stones can be divided into two artistic periods, the division occurring in 1971, when the Stones established their own record company and developed some control of their own recordings. We could obviously say that they had a 1960s period and a 1970s period, but even in the former, they reflected attitudes which would be vogue in the 1970s.

The period of the 1960s was largely spent in competition with the Beatles, although it was a competition of different energies. It must be understood that the Rolling Stones were great admirers of the Beatles and vice versa. However, comparisons were made and, in some ways, were helpful to the Stones, who after all started a little bit later than the Beatles. The Rolling Stones became a significant group in the mid-1960s, whereas the Beatles had become worldwide in importance by that time.

The Rolling Stones were highly individualistic. The major difference between them and the Beatles arose from the kinds of music which influenced them. The Stones were most influenced by rhythm and blues (in particular Chuck Berry), although skiffle may have been a minor influence. They took their name from a Muddy Waters' song, and during their formative years they played mainly blues. They were probably more technical than the Beatles in the beginning, and they seemed to have little concern for pretty melodies. Throughout their career, they were and still are hard rock musicians, and even when they sang songs originally designed as love songs, they sounded angry. Their roots are more in the shouting tradition than in crooning.

The story of their early career is parallel in some ways to the careers of Bill Haley and Elvis Presley, the giants of the 1950s. The Stones' career was shaped around the concept that they were tough guys, primarily as a contrast to the image of the Beatles. Rhythm and blues has an earthy quality, which is what made Presley so fascinating. The Stones also had this quality, singing black music in a black style, even though they were white. They left the sexual meanings in their songs and emphasized them with body language and their general behavior. They purposely manifested the decadent in society and

The Rolling Stones *(United Press International Photo)*

were justly condemned for it. However, nothing did more to build their early career than the condemnation of society.

As the press began to take up arms against the Rolling Stones and their public behavior, they developed a cult following. In 1963 and 1964, they recorded compositions by Chuck Berry, the Beatles, and Buddy Holly. These were successful in England, and in 1964 their first album was produced. In 1964, they had their first tour in America, which was quite successful, if only for the riots it caused. It must be understood that the Rolling Stones had a certain magnetism because they were English, but they were different from the Beatles in that they were completely unacceptable to the middle class. Although the Beatles were strange, they were at least cute. There has never been anything cute about the Stones.

Until 1965, they recorded material written by other people. However, from 1965 on they produced their own material and established themselves as the bad boys of rock. "Satisfaction" in 1965 was probably their first important song, in that it validated their earthy message. This particular song has a blues basis, but it carries the blues style into another sphere. It is sexual but it is also decadent sexuality. It has a riff orientation; we hear the main words until it feels as if they were pounded into our heads. It is negative in context, conveying the futility of trying in an age where nothing is in control. In my estimation, "Satisfaction" was the first punk rock tune.

From 1966 on, the Rolling Stones experienced legal problems. They were constantly being arrested for possessing drugs, and the press coverage made instantaneous heroes and villains of those involved. Mick Jagger and company became antiheroes for a society which treasured those kinds of things at that time — and their music continued to reflect that mood. They were involved with mysticism and psychedelics and were generally self-destructive. In short, everything they did was wrong, but it continued to build their image.

Their music in the late 1960s was good loud rock, but always combined with some catchy idea, either sexual or antiestablishment. One of their most significant, although less successful, albums of this period came out in 1967 — *At Their Satanic Majesties Request*. It was overshadowed by the Beatles' *Sgt. Pepper's Lonely Heart's Club Band*, but the Stones' album contains some of the best mystical rock ever. The evil side of mysticism is aptly covered. Whereas *Sgt. Pepper*'s tends to be optimistic and Messiah-like, the Rolling Stones do the same thing from the point of view of the devil. Again, although it was not a blatant competition, the Rolling Stones always managed to force the comparison by doing pretty much the opposite of what the Beatles did.

We should remember that the music of the Rolling Stones was technically quite excellent. In the later 1960s, they had psychedelic characteristics, even to a heavy metal or acid sound. It was strong rock with a blues base, which is what caused many people to say with awe that they may not like the people, but they played awfully good rock.

In the 1970s, the second period, they continued to perform some of the same kinds of music, but by this time they had perfected the model. The stylistic characteristics of the second period were not radically different from the first, but they were generally conceived in a purer way. The Stones continued to spit out the words and scream at us as they did in "Satisfaction," but by the 1970s they were doing it with gusto and consistency. Brian Jones, who died in 1969, was replaced by Mick Taylor, who was replaced in 1974 by Ron Wood from Faces. The technical expertise of the band got even better. Mick Jagger became the undisputed leader of the group and a cult figure through films and clothing styles. He had a major impact on trends in the 1970s, and it is largely for this reason that we consider him and the Stones to be that decade's image.

The Rolling Stones are important for their longevity and for being prototype punk musicians way back in the 1960s. However, they reflect a negative view, which is why we consider them representative of the 1970s. Add the fact that they play well, and the Rolling Stones must be taken seriously as a major group.

The Who

This group was made up originally of Roger Daltrey, Pete Townshend, and John Entwistle. They were later joined by drummer Keith Moon, who died in 1978; Moon was replaced by Kenny Jones of Faces. The band's original name was the Detours, which was changed to the Who by one of their early managers. The original concept of the Who in the mid-1960s was to be a mod band, which was quite different from other rock bands in London at that time. The mods were a subculture of people who dressed in outlandish and avant-garde ways. Although the music that seemed to thrive in a mod environment was rhythm and blues, there were many contradictions in its use. The mods were contemporary people who in some sense were part of high society, analogous to the people who followed be-bop jazz in the late 1940s and 1950s.

The term *mod* comes from clothing styles and is of course derived from the word *"modern"*. But more than simply reflecting a style of dress, mods were people who wanted to be ahead of their society. By definition, it is an urban movement, and in the case of England, it was found primarily in the high society of London. Most mods were fairly young or at least young at heart, and those who assimilated this style tried to set themselves apart from the rockers, that is, people who liked rock and roll. The distinction may have been artificial but it was viable. The Who began as a mod band that played in pubs in London.

One of the trademarks of the Who has always been a purposeful chaos. Even in the beginning of their career, the members were a disparate group, playing in a way which was abnormal. The function of each musician within the ensemble was not clearly defined, because the basic concept of mod was a form of anarchy. The drummer played in a sporadic manner, beating his drums like he was rebelling against society. The guitarist, Pete Townshend, was a power player, using the instrument like a battering ram. Although we are tempted to make the obvious comparison with acid or metal rock, Townshend's form of power was really quite different. It was not used to set up a psychedelic or other-world trip but rather to make a strong statement about the world as it really was.

The Who established itself as a band dedicated to the ridiculous, or perhaps even the absurd. The musicians did many of the things which would become trademarks of punk bands later in the 1970s, such as marching in place, jumping up and down, twirling the mike on its cord, turning the guitar against the amplifier for purposeful feedback, even smashing instruments. They were destructive first for attention and then finally as a statement in itself.

We have always taken seriously the image of a rock group or an individual musician. However, most of the musicians we have discussed were really rather flexible in the kind of music they performed. Seldom did they set themselves against the mainstream in quite the way that the Who did in the first part of their career. Whereas most musicians would play ballads or freely adapt their style to whatever would work at the time, the Who did not. They stuck to the style of being outlandish, before it was chic to do so.

Much of the early music of the Who could be dismissed as that of four musicians who were covering for their inability to play. However, they were all accomplished musicians by the time they got together. Intriguingly, they had little in common with each other, and this became their trademark: people playing together who had different ideas and at times did not even like each other. Their controlled chaos was a rallying point, and like the Rolling Stones, they established a cult following.

Some of the early music important in establishing the Who's style is found in the albums *I Can't Explain* (1965), *My Generation* (1966), *A Quick*

Elton John

The third representative of the 1970s in England, Reginald Kenneth Dwight, was born in Pinner, Middlesex, on March 25, 1947. He grew up as a relatively uninteresting person, even by his own admission. He was chubby, and except for his interest in playing the piano, rather bland. During his teenage years, he showed little interest in anything other than the piano, and his mother and stepfather encouraged him to become a musician. He began playing engagements with a rhythm and blues band, named Bluesology, when he was sixteen. At this time he was strictly a piano player and really never dreamed that he would be a singer, much less a rock star. It was not until 1969 that he began to be successful.

Through an audition for new talent, Elton John met Bernie Taupin, who was a lyricist. After John had composed music to Taupin's lyrics for some time, he and Taupin began to search for a producer. The first album produced in England, *Empty Sky* (June 1969), was not tremendously successful. However, their second album, entitled *Elton John* (April 1970), was, and one cut from that album, "Border Song," was especially successful. Although the song was not a record breaker, it has been sung by a number of other musicians, including Aretha Franklin. *Tumbleweed Connection* (October 1970) was also quite successful, both in England and in America, and by this time John had established himself as a major artist.

His dominance as a star occurred between 1970 and 1975. The following albums were significant during this time: *Friends* (1971), *Madman Across the Water* (October 1971), *Honky Chateau* (May 1972), *Don't Shoot Me, I'm Only the Piano Player* (January 1973), *Goodbye Yellow Brick Road* (October 1973), and *Captain Fantastic and the Brown Dirt Cowboy* (June 1975). Albums after *Captain Fantastic* were best sellers almost automatically, which is not to say that they were not also good. Playing the part of the local lad in the 1975 movie of *Tommy* helped John's career. He is today a viable artist, and although his interests have diversified, he is still an incredible performer.

There is some debate among rock critics about Elton John's talent, but we propose the following reasons for including him among the superstars: (1) He is a very proficient piano player. (2) He writes incredibly compelling melodies. (3) His singing style is both strong and sensitive. (4) He emotes expressive qualities through his singing. (5) The songwriting team of John and Taupin has been long lasting, although it decayed toward the end of the 1970s. (6) He understood the importance of theatrical performance and played the role to the hilt. Also, he has responded to his stardom in a socially redeeming way, in that he has not been afraid to enjoy his riches and indulge both himself and his friends by spending his money.

As a person, Elton John is most interesting. Physically, he is rather unimpressive, that is, without his outlandish clothes, hats, and glasses. Probably the most significant part of his stage look (which pervades his life) is the gimmick of his glasses. He has used all sorts of spectacles, including giant-sized ones. Those have become an Elton John trademark and have added immensely to his following. He has been called the Liberace of the rock world, and perhaps rightly so. Like Liberace, he also happens to be a fine musician. The extra items simply add to his aura, which is considerable.

It seems as if some critics have been so annoyed by his look that they

Elton John *(United Press International Photo)*

have failed to listen to his music. Elton John has succeeded in developing a persona as a musician in order to enhance the product. However, if he had not succeeded in producing real music, he would not have been successful on the basis of the extras. Elton John is a captivating performer, either live or on record.

We will examine one tune (and suggest that readers apply these techniques to other tunes) to discover the consistent musicality of the Elton John/Bernie Taupin team. One of the songs from *Caribou* (June 1974) — "Don't Let the Sun Go Down on Me" — was nominated for a Grammy. This is extremely powerful music, and John's melodic line is well worth whatever failures the album might contain. (In fact he was generally criticized for the album.) This particular song has been recorded by other rock artists; it has also been recorded by the Maynard Ferguson band. It would not have enjoyed this success had it not been good music. Like many of John's compositions, it is strongly written and quite compelling.

Elton John epitomizes the best of 1970s music, especially in the early 1970s. Like the late 1950s and early 1960s, this period was fairly devoid of new movement in rock. The Beatles were finished and so was the 1960s. With the exception of a few artists, the 1970s reflected a retrenching in rock, and John helped to fill the void. It was a time of commercialization, and the rise of disco from soul illustrated that rock had lost some of its purity and energy. John had a creative energy unsurpassed at that time, and he was also successful financially.

Probably the most interesting subordinate theme of John's music is the interest of Bernie Taupin in the old-fashioned, in particular the Old West of America. Although they were very English, they were both intrigued by America. Country and western influences are present in many of their collaborative works, and even if the music does not always sound like it, at least the lyrics and themes are influenced by country. It is ironic that country music maintained an active influence on rock in the 1970s, for example, on Led Zeppelin.

Although John was most significant up to 1975, he has remained active and is not yet nostalgic. He is still progressing, and he is far from ancient. Like all rock stars who pass the age of thirty, he has become old by conventional standards. He is no longer the new sensation, but he remains a genius in the context of his time. Although some critics have suggested that his singing is mechanical and nonexpressive, I believe this charge to be false. Elton John expresses his words in the context of the melodic and musical line, and within the appropriate context, his singing is both expressive and musical.

SUMMARY

In this chapter, we have considered three representatives of English music in the post-Beatles era. These musicians capitalized on the attitudes of the times with the amount of taste then required, which sometimes meant that they were tasteless and/or antiestablishment. Artists who are on the cutting edge of the changing attitudes of society are often misunderstood, and we must be quite careful in making value judgments. The main point is whether they were successful, whether people eventually understood them, and whether they had the strength of their convictions (proven by maintaining their position over time). All three of these representatives did, and therefore they must be considered relevant.

But perhaps more important, these representatives influenced others, both in England and in America. We have traced the impact of the Rolling Stones and the Who on punk and eventually new wave. Elton John proves the lasting impact of a pianist and vocalist and the efficacy of fusion music. Underneath his music lies a solid vein of good technique, which became paramount in the 1970s. The music may be simple, but it must be played accurately.

CHAPTER TWELVE

Folk and Eclectic Rock

In this chapter, we will consider two kinds of rock that were highly significant in the early 1970s — folk-rock and eclectic rock — although both movements began in the 1960s. The similarity of the two distinct forms is slight from a musical perspective, but they provided some of the elements from which fusion music arose in the 1970s (the subject of the next two chapters). As rock searched for a new creative identity, these two forms provided much of the material with which to experiment.

In the discussion of folk-rock, we will consider three eras of folk music, ending in the early 1970s. In the discussion of eclectic rock, we will treat three representatives of the style, which are, by definition, individualistic.

FOLK-ROCK

Folk music is usually defined as the music of the people, the folk's music. It is normally regionalistic, in that it expresses the feelings of one particular area or one particular group. It is most commonly simple music, and except for styles like bluegrass, it is vocal in orientation. The words are more significant than the music, although they are normally set to beautiful melodies. The music is repetitious, allowing many verses to be sung to the same tune. Although it has quite often been adapted to other styles, such as the blues or Dixieland, folk music is usually thought of as a separate art, and its practitioners see themselves as folk musicians. The music is generally not commercial in its pure form.

Whenever folk music takes on popular dimensions, that is, commercial value, it is usually because the particular themes being expressed have meaning for the society at that time. And whenever folk music becomes mixed with other forms, it is usually because the individual musician responsible wants to speak to a larger audience. Folk-rock represents the attempt by folk musicians to raise the consciousness of the rock audience. Only later in the development of this particular marriage of rock and folk do rock musicians use folk techniques.

Folk music has enjoyed a relatively separate audience through the ages, and the times had to be just right in order to mix that audience with one for rock — which was not to occur until the mid-1960s. Folk music could be traced back to the settlement of the United States. Much of what we said about slave music could easily be applied to folk music. There was black folk music, and there were white forms of folk music. For our purposes, the folk music before the eighteenth century is not too interesting because it was derivative of European styles. However, beginning in the late eighteenth century, there were waves of migration to the United States by different cultural groups, all developing and enjoying their own folk styles. Although we will not seek to trace each different form, we could illustrate the folk music roots of Irish, German, Italian, and other national groups as they moved to the United States. Each one developed a regional style of folk music and eventually added to the variety of American music.

The most interesting forms of folk music were the Southern style (Appalachian), the Western style (Texas-Mexican and country and western), and a combination of ethnic styles from the North. Of course, each of these various branches of the folk music form has a different audience and different subjects, although musically they are very similar. Broadly speaking, these various styles provided the musical material for folk singers in the twentieth century.

Although there were many significant folk singers before 1960, two of the most important were Woody Guthrie and Pete Seeger, at least in terms of influence. Although Guthrie was from Oklahoma and clearly reflected Southern styles, he was a spokesman for middle America in general. He sang many songs from the folk-blues tradition, but his most important contribution was as a social commentator. He was one of the first political commentators among musicians, and he became a folk hero in the early 1960s, when he was dying. His son, Arlo, is famous in his own right, particularly for "Alice's Restaurant."

Pete Seeger is also significant in any discussion of folk music. His father, Charles Seeger, was an eminent musicologist, and the son developed an interest in collecting folk music very early in life. He traveled with Alan Lomax, also a musicologist and anthropologist, and in these travels he absorbed many of the regional styles of folk music. Perhaps no other folk musician spent as much time in learning about the tradition as Seeger did. He is still productive in writing about the American scene and his background (travels and a Harvard degree) has made him singularly capable of articulating American views through words and music. His politics are liberal, and he has given us tunes like "We Shall Overcome" and "Where Have All the Flowers Gone?"

With these two musicians as important predecessors, we can turn our attention to the folk musicians of the 1960s, who were for the most part protest singers. Although each of their styles was different, they all learned from Guthrie, Seeger, and others. Some critics described the folk music of the 1960s as *new wave*, but it was musically derivative of earlier styles, just as new wave music in the late 1970s was partially derivative. However, the message was a bit more obvious than it was in music before that time.

Folk music in the 1950s was either pure folk music, sung by one person who accompanied him- or herself on guitar, or that sung by folk groups like the Kingston Trio. In other words, it was either folk music or it was pop music. The folk music of the 1960s combined the two styles in such a way that it had the power of the folk groups with the message of the individual singer.

Bob Dylan was the big story of the 1960s. However, he was a product of a particular time, and without the support of several other musicians, important in their own right, he would not have been as famous as he was. All of the following influenced Dylan and were in turn influenced by him.

Joan Baez preceded Dylan in popularity, becoming famous in 1959. She was a strong singer who identified herself very early with protest. She was against the Vietnam War and was antiwar in general. She was a constant participant in the student movement, especially in Berkeley in the early 1960s. She sang many of Dylan's tunes before Dylan himself had become famous. She and Dylan worked together for years, and they were inseparable at folk extravaganzas. Baez was one of the first really significant female folk singers of the 1960s, predating Janis Joplin and Grace Slick. She did not record with a rock band until the 1970s, but her style of singing led to a folk-rock form.

Joni Mitchell was important to the development of folk-rock because of her singing style and the way she used her backup musicians, one of whom was Stephen Stills. As her career progressed through the late 1960s and 1970s,

Joan Baez in concert, 1972 *(Photo by Willard E. Shattuck)*

she constantly expanded the form by adding rock and jazz. She has become quite proficient on several instruments and illustrates well the development of a folk singer into a folk-rock musician.

Peter, Paul, and Mary was an important group for two reasons: it was extremely popular, and it popularized the music of other, less well-known, musicians. The three were all good musicians, and of course they were excellent performers. The vocal blend they achieved would later be copied by other musicians — like Crosby, Stills, Nash, and Young — to produce complex textures within a rock sound. The significance of Peter, Paul, and Mary was that they were a symbol for the entertainment of the 1960s. Even when they sang protest songs (Dylan's included), they did it within a context of entertainment. When they sang children's songs, they evoked feelings of childlike behavior. Although they generally conveyed happiness, they were communicating to a generation of Americans who were deeply concerned.

Judy Collins was a classically trained pianist, but while in college in Colorado she began to perform as a folk singer. The rising political consciousness of the times began to affect her, and she soon found herself performing at protest meetings, singing music of other young folk singers. She was much more versatile than other musicians mentioned in this chapter, being involved in acting, films, and musical fusion. She made extensive use of electronic devices in rock and folk, also including classical and jazz influences.

But of course the most important was Bob Dylan. Born Robert Zimmerman in Duluth, Minnesota, he made his singing debut in Minneapolis while a student. He left Minnesota in 1961 and went to New York, where he became famous rather quickly. His first effective recordings were folk songs of the new left, exactly in the mold of Woody Guthrie. His two main themes were antiwar and antibigotry. His style was heavy, almost shouting in style, but from a folk-singing perspective. He was deeply imbued with blues styles, but not the shouting rhythm and blues style at all; rather, it was pure folk. Dylan's early popularity was completely tied to the 1960s and to the protest movement. He was a significant musical phenomenon because he represented commitment to an ideal. His singing style made it impossible to miss the message because it had no pop overtones. In fact, Dylan has seldom reached into the pop bag at all, with the exception of some funk tunes later in his career.

Of major significance is his performance with the Paul Butterfield Blues Band at the 1965 Newport Folk Festival. This marriage of a folk singer with a rock band was probably the major catalyst of the folk-rock tradition. Subsequent performances with the band identified the style of folk-rock, for which Dylan was responsible. At first people were negative, believing that Dylan had sold out to commercialization. However, in retrospect we can see that this was a perfectly normal kind of evolution. It made the message of the folk style even more powerful. Rock was the perfect backdrop for vocal-oriented music, providing an effective and interesting background.

It should be pointed out that Dylan was responsible for raising the level of sophistication of the lyrics. Some critics have said that Dylan is ultimately not very musical and that most of his significance comes from his lyrics, which are really fine poetry. It is certain that Dylan's poetry will have lasting impact. However, the fact that he chose to convey it through musical form makes him a part of the minstrel tradition, which conveys messages through words set to music. No serious consideration of the significance of lyrics in rock would be complete without an appreciation of what Dylan did to raise the standards. Although he may have been a product of the 1960s, his influence

Peter, Paul, and Mary in a reunion concert, 1979 *(Photo by Barry Rankin)*

Bob Dylan *(Used by permission of Fred Reif, Black Kettle Records, Saginaw, Michigan)*

Bob Dylan *(Courtesy of Columbia Records)*

extended well into the 1970s and beyond. We can hear his influence on many musicians of importance and in the significance of the words in much of the music of the 1970s.

Several bands in the late 1960s used folk music within a light rock style. These groups could be considered commercial responses to the folk-rock tradition, which began in the 1960s.

The Fifth Dimension was a black singing group which began in the early 1960s. It was basically a soul group at first, but it crossed over into the folk-rock market without being identified as a strictly black group. It toured with Ray Charles and had a number of hits. Its music was technically well done, which may be due to its association with Ray Charles. It used musical contrast well, and the combination of two women and three men was very bright. It has remained active throughout the 1970s and into the 1980s.

The Lovin' Spoonful, a rock band from the 1960s, was folk-oriented. John Sebastian, the leader, was a collector of folk music, and before the Lovin'

The Fifth Dimension in 1981 *(Courtesy of the Sterling/Winters Company)*

Jimmy Seals *(Photo by Barry Rankin)*

Spoonful, he was in several blues groups. His band, although short-lived, was extremely interesting if for no other reason than its diversity. The musicians were involved in writing film scores and recorded music for Frank Zappa's record company. Sebastian as a single continues to have a minor cult following.

The Mamas and the Papas grew out of the same band as the Lovin' Spoonful, but its later identification was different. It was a hippie band and basically a folk-rock group; except for their clothes, the members of the group were really not very psychedelic. Probably the biggest thing about the Mamas and the Papas was Cass Elliot, who died in 1974. The sound of this group was all vocal harmony, and its music was pure folk music with a light rock background.

Seals and Crofts was a vocal duo from Texas which enjoyed success in the early 1970s. At first, they had been Tex-Mex rock musicians; however, after some religious changes, they became folk musicians. When they came out with *Seals and Crofts* they quickly achieved some prominence. At first they just sang by themselves, although later they used a light rock sound as a backup. They represent a style which combines acoustic sounds (nonamplified guitars) with a folk-rock context.

Dash Crofts *(Photo by Barry Rankin)*

One last example from the 1960s should certainly be Simon and Garfunkel, who were both good musicians. Paul Simon, who later performed by himself, is an effective writer and is certainly responsible for some big hits during his career, most notably "Mrs. Robinson." Although they used only light rock backgrounds, if at all, they were important in that they commercialized the art form and discovered many clever ways to make statements about society without offending anyone. Their music is for the most part watered down in its impact, but it is very well done and the total package is compelling.

Most influential in the creation of a true folk-rock form in the 1970s was a 1960s group called the Byrds. The Byrds were formed in Los Angeles in 1964. The leader, Roger McGuinn, had been a part of the backup group for Judy Collins and also for Bobby Darin. David Crosby was one of the original members, joined by Gene Clark, Chris Hillman, and Michael Clarke on drums. The Byrds were an unusual southern California group, at least at the time. They imitated the Beatles although their music was not lyrically like that of the Beatles. They sang material by Dylan and also the Fifth Dimension, and although their music was derivative, they were successful. From 1965 to 1967 they used mostly folk-rock material, and after 1967 they began to fall apart. What is important about the Byrds is that it was a folk group, especially in the texture of the sound. It also contributed its members to various country-rock bands of the 1970s — the Flying Burrito Brothers and the New Riders of the Purple Sage.

Buffalo Springfield enjoyed some moderate success during its short-lived career (1966 to 1968) and later in re-releases of its albums. However, probably its most important contribution was as a proving ground for what would later become Crosby, Stills, Nash and Young (CSN&Y). The original Buffalo Springfield was made up of Neil Young and Stephen Stills; Richie Furay, who

Crosby, Stills & Nash   *(Courtesy of Atlantic Records)*

Crosby, Stills & Nash *(Courtesy of Atlantic Records)*

went to Poco; Dewey Martin, who became a soloist; and Bruce Palmer, who was deported to Canada. At one time, Jim Fielder played bass, but he eventually went on to Blood, Sweat and Tears. In short, Buffalo Springfield was not a stable group.

However, its musical concept was very stable in that it featured an acoustic sound with up to four independent vocal lines. The harmonies formed by the voices were very tight and served as a model for what CSN&Y would do later. The original compositions by Stills and Young, sung first by Buffalo Springfield, would form the stock of songs for CSN&Y — and in this fact lay the significance of Buffalo Springfield. It gave these two musicians a chance to work out their music within the controlled environment of the studio, and being in Los Angeles allowed them to work with the best of the available musicians. Jim Messina put in some time with them as well as other fine musicians from that area. For the development of folk-rock, Los Angeles was the studio location because of the availability of fine quality musicians, similar to Nashville's role in country music.

Crosby, Stills, Nash and Young was short-lived, but it was undoubtedly the most important group of the early 1970s. David Crosby was with the Byrds, Stephen Stills and Neil Young were with Buffalo Springfield, and Graham Nash was with the Hollies in England. It is interesting that the

Folk and Eclectic Rock

original collaboration took place at John Sebastian's house, where Crosby, Stills, and Nash combined to sing vocal trios. They subsequently decided to make albums together, putting out an extremely popular one in 1969. Neil Young joined them to form CSN&Y, after which they recorded *Deja Vu* in 1970.

The addition of Young allowed Stills to double on electric piano and synthesizer, and it also allowed for four independent vocal lines, a musical texture which had been tried in Buffalo Springfield. These four musicians were capable of singing very complex melodic lines, which became the cornerstone of the group's style. In some senses, CSN&Y illustrates the final stage of evolution for folk-rock. In this group, electronic devices were quite important, but only as backing for the vocal texture, the chief characteristic of folk music.

The actual musical sound of CSN&Y was a combination of acoustic guitar with lightly amplified electronic sounds. The chordal framework (that is, the progressions) was fairly complicated, and there was constant motion. The group had a continuous sound (perhaps reminiscent of surfing music), but the fluidity of the musical texture was quite a bit more complicated. It was soft rock in the sense that no one shouted and the words were always presented in a sophisticated texture. It was an organic sound rather than plastic. It grew with the words, that is, supported the words with musical textures appropriate to the text. The music of CSN&Y was very sophisticated, technically excellent, and communicated through a basic simplicity (that is, the complexity was disguised).

In conclusion, folk-rock has many different aspects. It was pure in the beginning, more folk than rock. The folk origins were couched in a political context, and when it was relatively pure, it was generally protest music. However, as the form became more sophisticated, there was the inevitable desire to make it speak to a larger audience. Rock, jazz, country, and other musical textures were added experimentally, ultimately leading to a fusion. Many of the musicians discussed in this chapter have used various musical media to expand their audiences, but most notably they have used rock forms. Therefore, rock combined with folk was a natural occurrence, which could have been predicted. The evolution of the form can be followed logically and explained chronologically. CSN&Y seems to be the logical conclusion. However, the influences of folk music on rock are still present and, for that matter, probably always will be.

ECLECTIC ROCK

Eclectic rock is a loose term which normally is applied to anything that is considered to be weird. In that sense, an awful lot of the music discussed in Chapter Fourteen might be described as eclectic. However, the real definition of the word describes the selection of that which seems best from a particular philosophy. Eclectic rock, then, is that type of music which tries to make a point about society without attempting any kind of commercialization at all.

It should be noted that when applied to specific groups, this is a value judgment at best. Many groups that might define themselves as eclectic would fall short of their self-imposed mission by actually selling albums or occasionally becoming commercial. However, it is generally possible to describe eclectic groups and to ignore their human frailties when and if they occur. We will attempt to provide an appropriate context for including certain musicians as eclectic, whether or not the musicians themselves would go to the point of calling themselves anything.

Some readers will simply define the following musicians as bad. That is a particularly dangerous kind of provincialism, although it is perfectly normal. It is sad that most highly experimental musicians (a quality of eclecticism) do not enjoy much success. In some ways, this is their contribution to the state of the art. That is, they are doing it for the sake of the art rather than for the sake of the money that they could earn if they were less dedicated.

The Fugs was a rock band formed in 1965 in Greenwich Village in New York City. The original group was made up of nonmusicians who were part of the avant-garde of New York. They were poetry-oriented — Ed Sanders also wrote a book on Charles Manson, called *The Family*; Tuli Kupferberg is a minor poet; Charlie Larkey, the bass player, married Carole King. As nonmusicians, they were somewhat like the Monkees, in that they formed a rock group for nonmusical reasons. However, unlike the Monkees, the Fugs had no financial motivation for becoming a rock group; they simply felt that this was the best way to communicate their messages.

The purpose of the Fugs was simply to shock for the sake of shock. They used blatantly gross obscenity, and rock was simply a background for obscene gestures and words. Their purpose was to shock society into realizing what was truth, and the medium they chose for the message was rock. Their music is at best chaotic, but it did have some influence on other groups who carried the philosophy further and perhaps did it better. One group, MC5, was influenced by the Fugs and became the prototype punk band.

Captain Beefheart represents an entirely different concept of an eclectic musician, in that he has had virtually no effect on anyone. Don Van Vliet (Captain Beefheart) is originally from California and went to high school with Frank Zappa. He formed the Magic Band in 1964, playing mainly blues with a number of very experimental electronic sounds. His techniques are avant-garde even when he is playing blues tunes. He uses rapid-fire lyrics with no rhyme scheme, multiple phasing, and special effects. He clearly mixes contemporary electronic music, jazz, and rock, as well as other kinds of music. He had gone back and forth between contemporary composition and blues performances. His career has been tied with the Mothers of Invention, even though he has his own band. The bottom line of his eclecticism (which is very much a part of the 1970s in attitude) is that he is thoroughly unpopular, and therefore successful as an eclectic.

The most significant proponent of the eclectic school of rock is Frank Zappa and the Mothers of Invention. Although he was born on the East Coast, Zappa moved to the West Coast at the age of ten and has remained there. He went to school in the desert in California, which probably affected him in some way. By the time he made his first album with the Mothers, called *Freak Out*, in 1966, he had been a lounge musician, in jail, a recording studio owner, and part of the Los Angeles underground. The first album, a complete story in itself, was a biography of the group and the scene of which it was a part. It was clearly a divergent view from the surfing scene or from that of the Byrds.

The first period of the Mothers ended in 1969, when Zappa disbanded it because of high costs. Probably the two most important albums from the early years are *Ruben and the Jets* and *Uncle Meat*, although Zappa fans might disagree. They were chosen here because they represent the two poles of Zappa's music. *Ruben and the Jets* is considered by some critics to be a sell-out because it so blatantly imitates 1950s rock and roll. However, Zappa's musical roots are in the 1950s, so it is not inappropriate for him occasionally to use an old blues melodic passage. Underneath the words, we can hear a constant parody of 1950s music. Zappa is laughing at the style, especially on cuts like "Deseri" and "Cheap Thrills." The sense of parody in Zappa — a style shared by the Fugs — is the strength of his eclecticism.

Uncle Meat, on the other hand, is serious composition. It is a studio album and would be difficult to perform in a live setting. Zappa's music is filled with other kinds of music — everything from Edgard Varèse to Thelonius Monk. Zappa is generally one of the best-educated rock musicians concerning other music, on a level with Pete Seeger. He is very progressive in the way that he mixes styles and uses sound on sound, such as crashes, crowds, and speeded-up sounds all at once. In "America Drinks and Goes Home," he is making a social comment and a musical comment through unusual sounds. In other songs, like "Plastic People," he utterly confuses us unless we are willing to give our complete attention to the various aspects of the music. Zappa does not record background music; his studio recordings are complicated, although his live performances (seldom done) are pretty simple in comparison.

In 1970, Zappa produced a movie called *200 Motels*, for which he wrote all the music. The movie is confusing and presents a mixture of images. Characteristically, it received very bad reviews. In 1971, he appeared with John Lennon and Yoko Ono in concert and put out two albums. *Waka Jawaka* in 1972 had George Duke on keyboards. After this album, Zappa returned to basic rock with strange lyrics. He predated punk by a number of years in his insistence on playing standard rock and roll of the 1950s. However, his rock and roll was not traditional because he always wrote lyrics of an antisocial nature. In 1975 and 1976, he toured again with Beefheart and then returned to studio work and touring with the Mothers.

Frank Zappa is the best of the eclectic rock musicians, in that he carries through one philosophy with great care. He was and still is an excellent guitar player and a gifted composer. He is learned in other musical styles, and although he has gone through a number of musicians over the years, he has commanded a sense of respect from the industry that he has condemned so soundly. In the beginning of his career, he advertised his records in comic books and through the underground; he also had numerous legal problems with the industry. However, in the end, Zappa has remained true to his ideals. His monumental set from 1979 and 1980, *Joe's Garage*, Vols. 1-3, illustrates that he is still creative, and he continues to influence musicians both in rock and in jazz.

SUMMARY

Both folk-rock and eclectic rock began in the 1960s and reflected societal views of that time. However, they went on to become major movements of the 1970s, with eclectic music continuing on into the 1980s. Attitudes in the 1970s were diverse, and these two types of music remained viable at a time when many different points of view could prevail. Even though they were worlds apart, their point of view was the same: to contrast markedly with the world of commercialism and sameness illustrated in the development of disco (which will be discussed briefly in the next chapter).

CHAPTER THIRTEEN

Jazz-Rock, Funk, and Disco

This chapter discusses fusion, which is the purposeful combination of two or more specific types of music. Because there were many attitudes prevailing at the same time in the 1970s, the idea of the art forms merging in something called fusion makes sense. Some people have suggested that fusion was logical because of the implications of technology, but it seems more likely that it came about because of diverse tastes. In any event, rock was heavily dominated in the early and mid-1970s by this particular concept. Rock was being influenced by and combined with other forms of music, and other forms were being affected by rock.

In some senses, rock has always been the product of other sources: first, rhythm and blues combined with white pop; later, big bands influenced the playing style. However, the intent of the performer and the desires of the audiences required a separate art form, one not tainted by certain influences. If the other forms were there, it was incidental to the rock music produced and not a part of the concept. In the 1970s, this was to change. Rock musicians became openly appreciative of other forms, studied them, and used their techniques blatantly.

This phenomenon actually started in the 1960s, although some other influential musicians had previously used jazz techniques, most notably Ray Charles. However, during the experimentalism of the 1960s, many musicians worked with other music. The Beatles were interested in Indian music, which they performed on recordings. Generally, many rock groups took advantage of electronic devices which had been created for jazz, like the electric piano and the synthesizer.

We will discuss eleven musicians and/or groups which identified themselves as jazz-rock musicians. Some of these musicians started before the 1970s, but jazz-rock as an important part of rock was totally a concept of that decade. In the funk section we will deal with musicians who were identified primarily with that movement. Funk as an outgrowth of soul or black music is also a concept of the 1970s. Finally, we will discuss briefly the significance of disco as a major phenomenon of that time, influential in many fields outside of rock. All three movements have strong jazz roots, although they clearly belong in the history of rock.

Fusion music of the 1970s has had enormous commercial impact, and all three types of music were financially successful. The results of commercialization in the history of rock were not always satisfying musically, but the result in the 1970s was music which both communicated and was artistically gratifying.

JAZZ-ROCK

As a jazz musician, I am biased toward this particular blending with rock. It has produced some very intriguing results, and in my opinion, the resultant music is stronger for the combination. It should be remembered that jazz and rock came from the same roots, and therefore that this particular marriage was one arranged from birth. The first issue to consider is why it happened at the time that it did.

The divergence of jazz and rock occurred in the early 1950s, when rock and roll became identified with an entirely different audience than that for jazz. Jazz was in some ways a separatist or elitist concept in the 1950s, and it was for the most part acoustic in performance. Whereas the rock musician relied heavily on amplification, the jazz musician shunned electronic devices. Jazz was either bohemian or progressive and sought higher planes of intellectual activity. Rock was basic and was aimed at a particular type of common person — young people and rebels. When and if jazz techniques were used by rock musicians in the 1950s, they were generally used by seasoned veterans like Ray Charles; but jazz was always a subtle influence, usually through gospel and rhythm and blues. We could trace the intervention of jazz styles into rock and roll (and vice versa) through the development of electronic wizardry, as well as through the technical ability of rock musicians.

With few exceptions, the rock musician of the 1950s was not technically a good musician. The musical technique required to imitate the style was not very complicated. Even the best of the musicians, Chuck Berry and Ray Charles, did not need technical expertise because the words were more important than the background.

The rock musician of the 1960s was not radically different in this respect, at least not until the end of the decade. The major artists were by and large singers who just happened to play an instrument. A few of the folk singers, Joni Mitchell for example, had technical ability on an instrument, but in their early recordings they did not show it. It simply was not necessary. What led to an expansion of technical ability was the experimentation of the 1960s coupled with an expanding interest in different textures. As musicians began to experiment with different combinations of instruments, they had to learn to play them well. Occasionally, this need caused musicians to practice technique simply for its own sake. Sometimes it produced fine players.

Also, sometime in the 1960s there was a subtle shift in musicians' attitudes. It may be that it was caused more by the media than anything else. As rock became more and more popular as a media phenomenon, especially on television, it was more and more necessary for studio musicians to be able to play in different styles. Although studio musicians seldom had the influence on other musicians' attitudes that they probably should have, from the mid-1960s on there was a change in this respect. Many people wanted to be complete musicians, especially as the role of the musician in society became more profitable and more diversified.

For many reasons, jazz musicians no longer thought it evil to play rock, and some fine jazz musicians began to do so, for example, Chick Corea, Herbie Hancock, and later, George Benson. These are musicians who in a previous generation might not have stooped to rock. However, in the 1970s, they made major contributions to both jazz-rock and the world of funk-pop.

Blood, Sweat and Tears (BS&T) was a tremendously significant rock group for many of the previously stated reasons. Under the able direction of Al Kooper on organ and synthesizers, the group used a horn section (like Chicago) with a more traditional rock rhythm section. The former was initially used like a rhythm and blues horn section in that it played punctuated riffs simply in order to add to the instrumental texture. Started in 1967, BS&T set a standard for jazz-rock. Although it was not kept up, the initial concept was to use jazz techniques under the surface of a rock band. The vocals were very important, as they were for Chicago. However, the most important characteristic of the music was that it was highly technical, far surpassing the general level of music in 1967. The most important aspect of jazz emphasized was the highly technical and difficult melodic line.

The Chicago Transit Authority, later shortened to Chicago, began in

Chicago in concert, 1980 *(Photo by Barry Rankin)*

1968 and was made up of musicians who were technically very competent. They used the same basic ensemble as BS&T, with the addition of a trumpet. Chicago combined rock with jazz interludes by the horn section. It was probably the first group to make extensive use of horn melodies and solos, which were real jazz excursions. It also experimented with shifts in accent and some very fine writing for the horn section. The group has enjoyed continued success as a result of its technically perfect performances, its strength as a rock group, and its feel for jazz.

Billy Cobham is a jazz drummer par excellence, born in Panama and raised in New York. He worked with Miles Davis during his formative years and subsequently became one of the most dynamic drummers around. He worked with John McLaughlin and has played in support of a diverse group of people, including James Brown and Herbie Mann. He is equally at home with jazz, funk, and rock. In my estimation, he is the Stanley Clarke of drummers, and the combination of his technical ability and his raw power made him an important example of the emerging jazz-rock musician of the late 1960s. His major significance as a jazz-rock drummer occurred in the 1970s.

Chick Corea is a New-York raised Puerto Rican, best known as a jazz pianist. However, most of his jazz is heavy funk or is Latin influenced. Corea is a very versatile musician, especially good at improvisation; he makes extensive use of electronics and synthesizers. He has experimented heavily with unusual meters and chord changes. Although he is perhaps not well known to the rock world, in his jazz performances he plays some of the best rock around. Primarily a phenomenon of the 1970s, he continues to influence people in this decade.

Chicago *(Photo by Barry Rankin)*

Earth, Wind and Fire is slightly different from the previously mentioned musicians, but it is quite clearly a jazz-funk group. Started in Chicago in 1971, the group uses an expanded rock ensemble — multiple percussion and extensive keyboards (organ, piano, and synthesizers) — and one horn player doubling on flute, tenor sax, and soprano sax. Again, these are very technical players who use the funk sound to great effect. Although many of the jazz-rock

Earth, Wind, and Fire   *(Courtesy of Columbia Records and Bruce W. Talamon, photographer)*

groups are clever in their use of dynamics and staging, Earth, Wind and Fire is one of the best. One of the most delightful characteristics of this group is its ability to keep the feel going, changing from loud to soft instantaneously.

Electric Flag had the shortest career of any significant jazz-rock group. It was formed in 1967 and established itself at the 1967 Monterey Festival. It was the first group to use two horn players in a rock context, and although it lasted less than two years, it was very influential because of the musicians' technical virtuosity.

Emerson, Lake and Palmer was not a jazz-rock group, but it was influential on that style. This trio used jazz improvisation techniques in creating fusion music that combined rock with classical. The best example of this type of fusion is their version of Modest Mussorgsky's *Pictures at an Exhibition*.

Herbie Hancock is another jazz musician who has bridged the gap between jazz and rock, primarily through funk. A concert pianist, Hancock was classically trained and schooled in the real world at the same time. He was the pianist for Miles Davis between 1963 and 1968 and is highly regarded

Keith Emerson *(Courtesy of Atlantic Records)*

Greg Lake *(Courtesy of Atlantic Records)*

Carl Palmer *(Courtesy of Atlantic Records)*

for his improvisational ability. He is equally at home with electronic keyboards or synthesizers and with the acoustic piano. He is probably most famous for his composition "Watermelon Man" and has been voted the best pianist by *Downbeat, Playboy*, and other polls. He and Chick Corea are the two most important pianists in the jazz-rock tradition.

John McLaughlin is an English guitarist who first succeeded as a virtuoso jazz guitar player. He played with Miles Davis on his *Bitches Brew* album of 1971. In the latter part of that year, he converted to a Bengali mystical religion and subsequently developed two different avenues of musical communication. One was Indian music, played mainly on acoustic guitar; the other was a pulsating jazz-rock. He formed the Mahavishnu Orchestra, which was an expanded ensemble reaching symphonic proportions at one time. His jazz-rock music is very powerful, and even within the context of traditional Indian music, his virtuosity is obvious. Of the jazz-rock guitarists, perhaps only George Benson rivals his talent.

Jean-Luc Ponty is a French violinist who was classically trained. He became a significant jazz violinist in Europe and ultimately performed in the United States, where he played with the Mothers of Invention. As the amplified violin is rather a rarity, Ponty is without rival, with the possible exception of Papa John Creech.

Santana is an important representative of the jazz-rock school, especially in its blending of Latin-American elements. Carlos Santana was the son of a *mariachi* musician and spent his formative years playing in Tiajuana, Mexico. He moved to San Francisco during the height of the youth culture and firmly established his band in the late 1960s. He employed many Latin-American musicians, and his major compositions were Latin in flavor. Probably his most important album was *Abraxas* in 1970. In the mid-1970s he worked with John McLaughlin and later with Alice Coltrane, John Coltrane's wife. Santana deserves credit as a great musician, and within the context of his various bands the sound was effective, with obvious Latin and funk overtones.

Weather Report was formed in 1970, and the two important members of this group are Josef Zawinul on keyboards and Wayne Shorter on saxophone. Both musicians are alumni of Miles Davis. Zawinul is a classically trained pianist from Vienna, Austria, and Wayne Shorter is a black saxophonist from the East Coast. Both are phenomenally good jazz musicians who moved slowly into the jazz-funk school while retaining their excellent improvisatory abilities. *Heavy Weather* in 1977 was a smash hit with both the rock and jazz audiences; several tunes from that album have been covered by other jazz musicians, Sonny Rollins and Maynard Ferguson, for example.

The significance of jazz-rock is as follows:

1. Some very competent musicians began to make contributions to rock technique.

2. Rock became more complicated as a result.

3. The commercial value of rock was made broader by the inclusion of an audience that would previously have shunned it.

4. At times, the message of the lyrics was stated better because of the expanded support mechanism.

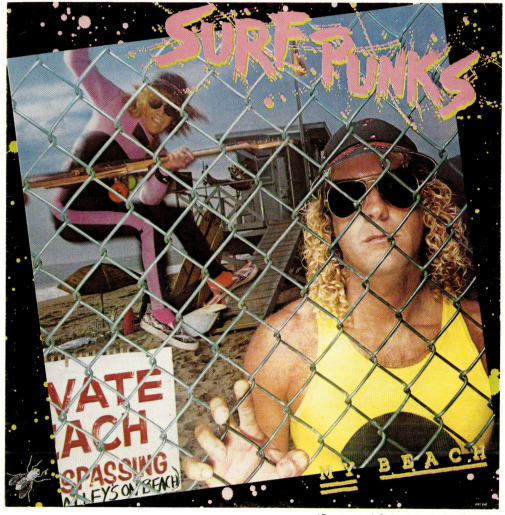

(Courtesy of Columbia (Epic) Records)

(Courtesy of Columbia Records)

(Courtesy of Columbia Records)

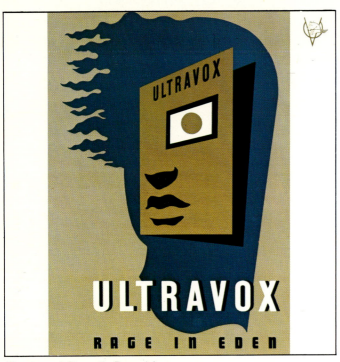

(Courtesy of Chrysalis Records)

(Courtesy of Columbia Records)

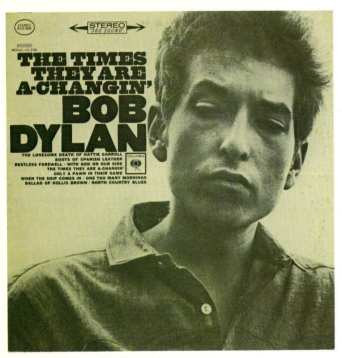

(Courtesy of Columbia Records)

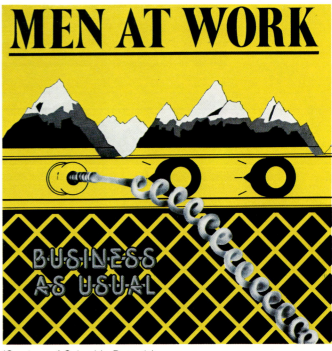

(Courtesy of Columbia Records)

(Courtesy of Capitol Records)

(Courtesy of Capitol Records)

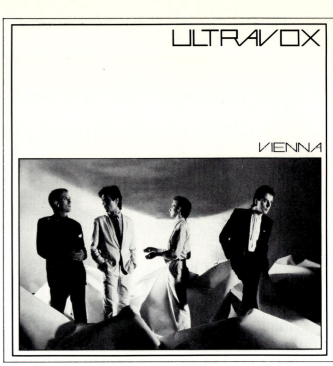
(Courtesy of Chrysalis Records)

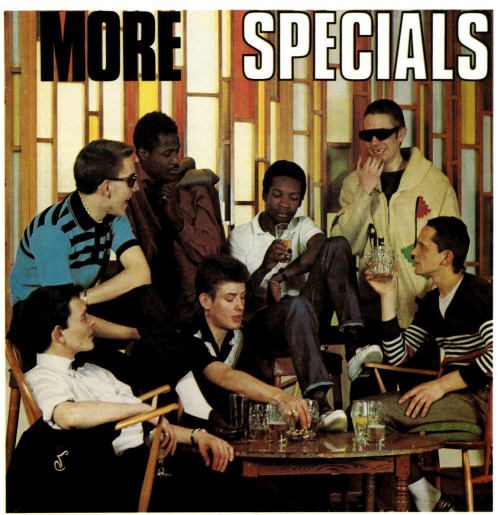
(Courtesy of Chrysalis Records)

Herbie Hancock *(Courtesy of Columbia Records)*

Carlos Santana *(Courtesy of Columbia Records)*

Weather Report *(Courtesy of Columbia Records)*

5. Many electronic devices became commonplace in both jazz and rock.
6. Studio musicians set the standard for musical development as the media demanded more of this type of music.
7. Jazz influences began further to legitimize rock as a serious form of communication.

Rock improvisation had been quite static until this period. Even though the result of the jazz-rock merger was more commercial music, watering down the basic prototypes, the music became technically more proficient in general; and in particular, rock improvisation began to take on aspects of jazz improvisation. It became more melodic, more expansive, and generally just more interesting. Whereas previously the guitar had been almost the only instrument to play solos, in the jazz-rock era the solo function was expanded to include keyboards and other melodic instruments. Saxophone solos of the 1970s (which were important in the 1950s) were more like jazz solos, and the technique required to play them was much more demanding. In all, jazz-rock has had an exhilarating effect on the development of rock musicality.

FUNK

The word *funk* can be defined in several ways, all of which are inaccurate. The most common way is to think of it as a four-letter word, which has various sexual and social meanings. Funk evolved from music called *soul*, which is a euphemism for black music. Soul was the term that replaced rhythm and blues in the black community, and soul music was most certainly centered in Detroit and the Motown (Motor Town)[1] complex of the 1960s and 1970s. Early soul music was personal and spoke clearly to blacks and their concerns. Funk did the same in its early stages.

The first recording which contained the word funk was Dyke and the Blazers' "Funky Broadway" in 1967. Of course earlier tunes contained the word, but this was the first recording successful enough to be played on the radio. As soon as the word was used, it was legitimized, and any evil implications were glossed over. Funk became a way of life, a feel for existence, especially within the black community.

However, funk is also musically definable, and it was not long before the style was copied by white musicians. By the early 1970s, funk was probably the most significant style in rock, and maybe in pop music in general. Funk certainly began as an expression of black consciousness, and the funk vocabulary is a specialized black vocabulary. Even with the separation of the black and white communities at that time, funk managed to become a bridge between them.

The funk style does not depend on any particular chord progression, although it was quite often played in the blues style. Some funk pieces do not change chords at all, because funk is a musical and rhythmic texture. Funk can be totally instrumental, although at first it was primarily a musical background for narrative songs. The funk style requires a particular rhythmic ensemble — percussion and bass line — and either sustained chords or rhythmic interpolations by other instruments. Like rock in general, it uses evenly spaced beats rather than a swing jazz feel and syncopation. Quite often, once the basic feel is established, it simply repeats the music over and over. The best general description of funk is the concept of "street feel" or the way one walks. Funk is an attitude, which when expressed musically transforms the listener into a particular mood, usually described as laid-back or mellow.

Funk can be aggressive, and its message can be bleak or depressing, depending on the times. However, the musical structure combines both softness and harshness. Backup instruments often come in as punctuated short riffs. The most common beat pattern for these punctuations is an accent on beat four of a four-beat measure (usually short-short-long). The beat pattern of the percussion group, the simplest being just a drum set, is rather constant but clipped short most of the time. Sustaining is the responsibility of either the voices or a keyboard instrument. Funk is electronic because it is an urban style.

Probably its most important musical feature is the bass line, and depending on the player, it can be quite complicated or relatively simple. To fully

---

[1] There is a separate history that could be told at this point, that is, the development of Motown music. We have included Motown in the general description of soul music and have mentioned that Detroit was its center. Obviously, we have left out many major musicians. However, our purpose has been to be appropriately representative, not encyclopedic.

appreciate the funk style, we must sort out the bass line. In simple styles, the bass line will set up a repetitive rhythmic pattern based on one and five of the musical scale; many funk tunes don't change chords at all, so it is easy to analyze them. If the tune is really complicated, it will usually be the result of a complex bass line. Stanley Clarke has enormously complicated funk bass lines, and in this style he is the undisputed master.

The history of black attitudes can certainly be heard in funk tunes, which are a minichronicle of black attitudes in the last fifteen years. In this sense, funk is very relevant to what the black community perceives as its position in society, and it is an interesting study in itself. The latest stage in the evolution of funk was probably the *rap*, a phenomenon of the late 1970s. This was a free-form conversation with lightly textured funk music in the background.

James Brown established himself in the late 1950s as a gospel and rock singer with remarkable strength. His singing style is that of a shouter, but his strength goes beyond that form. He has become tied to the black-power movement and in particular to the funk sound. In 1968, his "Say It Aloud — I'm Black and I'm Proud" became the standard bearer for the black power movement in general and funk music in particular. Of course, Brown was a gospel singer and still is, but he moved into funk before the word became fashionable, using Afro-American rhythms and jazz influences (in particular the riff orientation of rhythm and blues). He is an incredible entertainer and really preaches when he sings. He has been called everything from "the godfather of soul" to "the minister of new super heavy funk."

Kool and the Gang is a very successful East Coast group which put together all the funk elements into one unit. Its greatest success was in the early 1970s (especially 1974) with songs like "Funky Stuff" and "Jungle Boogie," although in the late 1970s it scored big with "Celebration." The funk background is remarkably versatile, and the voices sort of flow through the varied background. In general, the group is optimistic and always very mellow.

The Commodores started in the late 1960s, and in 1970 they were the opening act for the tour by the Jackson Five. Their first album was called *Machine Gun* (1973); one of the songs, "Do the Bump," was a crossover in that it was quite successful with a basically white audience. The Commodores use a standard rhythm section, saxophone, and trumpet. It is definitely a funk band, although its music fits nicely into the disco concept as well.

Parliament was a vocal group founded in the mid-1950s. The leader of this group and the one that evolved from it (the Funkadelics) was George Clinton, who is the purest of funk musicians. He believes in raw energy, which both Parliament and the Funkadelics had. Their style was mainstream funk with no commercial softening at all, and the vocal line was most important. They did little crooning like Kool and the Gang, and even funk-rock groups like Earth, Wind and Fire were criticized by Clinton as sell-outs. For real funk people, the Funkadelics (or Parliament-Funkadelic, as it is sometimes called) is the model for the form.

Like many of the different forms of music in America, funk has become a part of the necessary repertory of a musician. We cannot imagine professional musicians today not being able to play at least five or six funk riffs. However, once they know these five or six riffs, they can survive indefinitely. Funk is enjoyable to play but is quite simple. Unless it is mixed with jazz, it is technically not demanding. On the other hand, it can be rigorous, as played, for example, by Stanley Clarke.

Kool and the Gang *(Courtesy of PolyGram Records)*

DISCO

Disco, a movement of the 1970s, was very important — at least until the new wave — because it provided a central focus for the return to dancing. Other than Donna Summer, however, not many people have become successful solely from disco music. John Travolta, in *Saturday Night Fever*, established himself as a sex symbol, based on his disco dancing as well as his image. Even though a number of musicians — Kate Smith, James Brown, Diana Ross, Chuck Mangione, and the BeeGees, for example — have made disco recordings, the form has been unproductive for the creation of new, exciting music, although it has had some commercial success.

Disco is simply dance music with an even tempo and a light rock feel (in fact it is played rather consistently at one tempo — about 130 beats per minute). It often has funk undertones, but it is not as obvious or compelling as funk. Many of the funk performers have made disco recordings which lacked the smoothness disco requires. In some senses, disco is the Muzak of the rock world, and like Muzak it was at one time very successful.

Donna Summer in 1981 *(Photo by Barry Rankin)*

Donna Summer *(Photo by Barry Rankin)*

Chuck Mangione in concert, 1980 *(Photo by Barry Rankin)*

Diana Ross in 1980   *(Photo by Barry Rankin)*

Diana Ross *(Photo by Barry Rankin)*

The subject matter of disco is optimistic and without social comment. It is simply good-time music, sexually unobtrusive in the sense that all real emotions are guarded. Disco has returned to the platonic relationships of ballads in the late 1950s, although some of Donna Summer's disco songs have overtly sexual lyrics, such as "Love to Love You, Baby," "Hot Stuff," "Bad Girls," and "Dim All the Lights." It often suggests relationships or nostalgia toward some place, but always with a hint of optimism. It is a clear reaction to the growing complexity and sadness of the 1970s, and many people seek refuge in it.

There is no question that disco was the most commercial venture of the 1970s, a musical formula which could be applied evenly to anything. All a musician had to do was add a rock beat and smooth out the lyrics — the result was disco. Many types of music were changed into disco tunes, even some of the favorite cartoon songs of Walt Disney.

Disco has also had far-reaching implications for other types of music and the social scene. It has become part of the standard repertory, and we can expect to hear it in certain social settings. It has affected jazz. The opening song of Chick Corea's *Secret Agent* (1979) is a disco tune. The jazz-funk trumpeter Tom Browne uses disco very tastefully and effectively on his album *Tom Browne* (1980). Disco complements jazz nicely, as it bears much resemblance to the fast samba form. In fact, we might even argue that the disco beat, with accents on beats two and four, might have come from the samba and/or bossa nova.

Few stars emerged from disco because the form was not sustainable except for dancing. It was difficult, if not impossible, to reproduce its total effect in a concert because disco was designed for dance halls, with the lights, the action, and the people. It had become a DJ's art form in that what mattered was continuous music, and not necessarily recognizable music. Records were produced for discos which simply required a specific musical style and nothing else. Disco was responsible for taking jobs away from live musicians, so naturally it was not favored by professional musicians. However, all that aside, it was a valid response to a confusing world, and it did provide escape.

CHAPTER FOURTEEN

Punk and New Wave

This chapter attempts to draw together the main types of new music from 1977 to the present. This material is almost out of date the minute that it is written. Even rock critics have not yet had time to completely assess punk, much less new wave, but we can point out some generalities about the different forms and some of the people and groups who are important.

Like anything relatively new, punk and new wave have many detractors. However, we should approach this music with an open mind, the same as we have with older music. Although both punk and new wave are progressive movements, they have some elements in common with more traditional rock; thus, much of what we have learned up to this point can help us understand the newer music. Because we do not have all the listening skills necessary to understand it completely, however, a proper assessment will undoubtedly have to wait until punk and new wave are a part of history.

In the last part of the chapter, we will attempt to formulate some predictions about what musical forms will appear next. This is purely speculative and may be entirely wrong; but one of the points of this study is to collect information and trends with which we should be able to make a logical (even if ultimately incorrect) prediction. If the cyclic view of history is accurate, we should be able to predict the next turn.

PUNK

The term *punk* is usually applied to a child or teenager who acts in an antisocial way. It was also used to describe a particular clothing style in London in the 1970s, an updated version of the Teddies of the 1950s and the mods of the 1960s. Similar terms in the United States were *beatnik* and *hippie*. Punk was slightly different because it suggested being outside the law. However, the common element of all these types was that they were unconventional and antiestablishment.

Punk certainly started much earlier than the mid-1970s. There were punk qualities about Elvis Presley in his individualistic clothing styles and particularly in his hair. In the 1960s, there were many prototype punk musicians — the Rolling Stones, the Who, Frank Zappa, and others. Anyone who made strong statements and did outlandish things could be labeled a punk, before that term was applicable musically. Jimi Hendrix could be seen as punk because he was destructive, occasionally smashing a guitar on stage. However, these musicians were incipient punkers; they were not thoroughly dedicated to punk, which was simply a part of their entertainment package.

Punk was a form of rebellion, like other styles of rock; it turned against all other musical forms of the 1970s. Some critics saw it as an artistic movement, in this case antiart similar to that of the Fugs in the 1960s. It was the ultimate in sensationalism and should be seen as a philosophy of musical production, wherein the total statement was more important than the music and any constituent part of the performance.

Although punk was named after an English clothing style, the first real punk musician was Iggy Pop (James Jewel Osterburg), who was born in Ann Arbor, Michigan in 1947. It is interesting that Iggy Pop and the Stooges, MC5, John Cale, and the Velvet Underground were all performing at the end of the

1960s. Each reemerged in the 1970s as a new group. Iggy Pop and the Stooges was consistent in its punk style before that style became set. It was established by *The Stooges* in 1969 and *Fun House* in 1970 and eventually served as the model for punk groups. In these albums, the group used abstract lyrics and a repetitious background. Over the years, Iggy Pop has remained a crazy if not exciting musician, who more than once has been assisted by David Bowie, who many people feel is the godfather of punk.

The Sex Pistols, established in 1975 with the leader Johnny Rotten (Lydon), became the leader of the British punk movement. Sid Vicious joined the group on bass in 1977, and the combination of Vicious and Rotten set the group's tone, if only by name. In short, these were very nasty people.

It is interesting that many punk groups featured musicians who were mainly lyricists rather than strong instrumentalists. Before joining the Sex Pistols, Johnny Rotten had never sung in a band. Two groups mentioned earlier started out from the same perspective, the Fugs and the Monkees. The Fugs, you may recall, were basically poets who came together to express the values of Greenwich Village. They were new wave musicians because of that one factor.

The music of the Sex Pistols was raw and uncontrolled. The background music was reiterative, and the music itself was reminiscent of 1950s rock and roll, straight, continuous sound and four-beat drumming. Rhythms tended to be even and just slightly clipped off, a staccato (short) effect. However, the musical background was not the primary element; the image was all-important, and perhaps even the words were secondary. The purpose of punk was to shock, to hurt people's feelings, and generally to lay all emotions open, like a wound.

This was a conscious reaction to the 1970s, and it was perhaps a more honest reflection of it than any other kind of music at that time. In the mid-1970s, the world seemed to be falling apart. Economic disasters, hijacking, terrorism, and imminent war were all at hand. These, combined with runaway technology and the lack of individual control over events, caused great anger and frustration. Some people sought refuge in nostalgia (Sha-Na-Na and big bands), whereas others expressed themselves through punk rock.

The Sex Pistols, Iggy Pop and the Stooges, and Adam and the Ants were some of the punk bands who were made popular by the indignation of polite society and the hatred of the press. The Sex Pistols were banned from the radio and many public performances; this gave them cult status. They had learned their lessons from Mick Jagger very well. Like rockers as far back as Bill Haley, the Sex Pistols were successful because so many people hated them.

In England, they were followed by the Clash, the Damned, and others who copied their concept. Punk rock was primarily an urban concept, and, at least in England, it had significant impact. The chordal style and straight rhythms allowed the image and the lead singer to project the fundamental premise of punk rock — straight, ugly truth. Even the melodies were not highly significant, and although there was a blues influence, it also was incidental to the image. What was important was the way the musicians accosted their audiences. They danced around, quite often just jumping up and down (called the *pogo*), screamed, and made obscene gestures. They used extensive feedback and distortion.

The lead singer usually spit the words at the audience, and there was little or no rhyme scheme. The clothing and hairstyles were somewhat like

Adam Ant *(Courtesy of Epic Records)*

The Clash *(Used by permission of Laura Levine, photographer)*

those of the 1950s, although more style-oriented — leather jackets, short hair, and mean visages. Punk rockers were not known for their social graces and quite often built their reputations by nasty actions outside of their performances (especially in public places). For punk, they wore their hair with the wet look; for new wave, the dry look was in.

The United States had its share of punk groups, and for that matter, still does. The New York Dolls was managed by the manager of the Sex Pistols, Malcolm McLaren. The Ramones was a significant U.S. punk group. Although its success was not major, it was purely punk; it did not become new wave, which most other punk groups eventually did. Most of the other groups actually straddle the line between punk and new wave, some of the most notable being Blondie, the B-52s, the Talking Heads, Devo, and others.

NEW WAVE

It is essential to take new wave seriously because it contains within it a number of different kinds of musical groups, some of which are really quite excellent. We consider it to be a separate category from punk, although some people would call punk the first stage of new wave.

New wave refers to new music, like *ars nova* referred to music in the fourteenth century as opposed to *ars antiqua* of the thirteenth century. It is the same as using the word *contemporary* to describe that which is happening today.

New wave describes many different styles of music, but generally it is a philosophy of life which manifests itself in certain kinds of music. It encompasses music which is both complex and simple, old and new in structure, and positive and negative in feeling. If it is described as having "older" elements, it

Blondie   *(Courtesy of Chrysalis Records)*

Elvis Costello *(Courtesy of Columbia Records)*

The Talking Heads *(Scott Weiner/Retna Ltd.)*

must be understood that these are always within the context of the modern studio and technology of the 1980s. Although it may at times be repetitious and may also contain elements of punk, it is more encompassing than either older music or punk. There is an abstractness about new wave music which places it on an artistic plane. New wave is broader than a musical style; it is a philosophy of living in today's world, or perhaps, even tomorrow's.

Britain has been the leader of the new wave movement, even though we may have heard more new wave bands from America. Two important English musicians are Elvis Costello and Graham Parker. They both made the transition through pub music and punk to new wave. They brought to new wave an energy which included the anger of punk and the sophistication of other musical styles. The Clash is important for the same reasons because it was able to ride through the punk era and come out the other end as a formidable ensemble, with its own unique sound.

Some other important new wave bands from England are the Undertones, Stiff Little Fingers (Irish political music such as "Barbed Wire Love"), Gang of Four (actually Scotsmen), Magazine, the Buzzcocks, XTC, Stray Cats, and Wire. One aspect of new wave is called *ska*, which is Jamaican reggae music combined with a contemporary rock band. Some of the important ska bands are Madness, the Beat, the Selecter, and the Specials. Ska bands usually contain both white and black musicians. The Specials had a

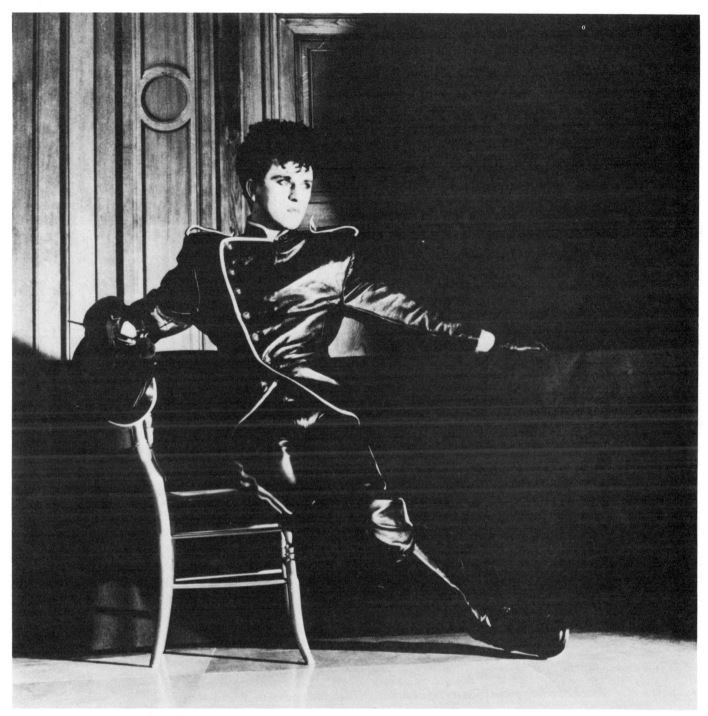

Visage *(Courtesy of PolyGram Records)*

big hit with a tune called "My Town is a Ghost Town," which talked about the riots in London. Although some of these bands may not be well known in America, they are all good musical groups with an amazing amount of creativity.

Probably the best American new wave group is the Talking Heads, which was mentioned in the section on punk. Although there are many new

Flock of Seagulls *(Courtesy of Jive Records)*

Men at Work *(Courtesy of Columbia Records and Laura Levine, photographer)*

wave bands in the United States, the Talking Heads is an especially attractive ensemble. Many of its compositions are African-derived with very complex rhythmic structures underlying a monochordal and monothematic singing style. Its lyrics have a contemporary message, and the music is the ultimate in fusion.

In the 1980s, new wave has definitely begun the process of bringing in other forms of music and has shown all the signs of becoming a broadening art form. New wave has no definitive musical characteristics because so much music is now referred to as new wave. Some of the most important movements in the 1980s have been the following: the *new romantics*, represented by Visage, Ultra-Vox, and at times Adam and the Ants; the *blitz* (essentially *disco-new wave*) is electric-chic-disco-oriented and is antipunk, represented by Flock of Seagulls, Men at Work, Soft-Cell, and Kraftwerk; *punk-jazz*, represented by its spiritual leader Ornette Coleman and bands like Material; and *blue wave*, a combination of blues and new wave, represented by the Fabulous Thunderbirds (Texas), the Blasters (California), and the Stray Cats (originally from New York but most successful in London).

New wave is definitely still alive and may continue to expand its territory. As a term basically meaning experimentation, new wave should not be understood as static but as growing. Some of it may ultimately be judged favorably by history, and undoubtedly some of it will not. The point is that it is viable art and is exhibiting growing influence and popularity.

THE FUTURE

In this chapter, we have outlined some of the attitudes that brought about punk and new wave and we have identified them as separate movements. That in itself may not be true, as it is truly debatable whether punk and new wave are separable, but the point for us is that punk quite naturally grew into new wave, and then new wave became the focal point for further expansion. The expansion is quite clearly a broadening of the art form, bringing in other forms of music, such as jazz and blues. This seems to fit a cyclic view of development within rock and roll and brings to mind similar developments in the 1950s, late 1960s and the mid-1970s.

We have not considered the continued development of mainstream rock and roll during this period and especially the development of heavy metal and funk-soul. Readers will undoubtedly wonder why Styx, Queen, Aerosmith, and many others have not been mentioned as pivotal to 1980s music. Although the popularity and vibrancy of mainstream rock is certainly significant to the art form, it probably is simply a continuation of somewhat older models, which have been covered earlier in the book. Punk and new wave were selected for discussion because they are new and provide new characteristics.

Keeping in mind that the 1980s have witnessed a shift to conservatism in both England and the United States, we predict a continued interest in the past (that is, in rock and roll in a relatively pure form). However, we can also see from previous cycles that there is a tendency for rock to solidify itself into one philosophical model and then to spread out, bringing in other sources. We have witnessed this in the early 1980s with new wave.

Therefore, we predict that new wave music is the fusion music of the early 1980s, as jazz-rock and disco were in the mid-1970s. After a few years of increased fusion, we will undoubtedly see a return to a purer model. If political history is any indication, this will probably occur at the time that there is a shift toward a liberal point of view. Since we had a return to 1950s roots in new wave at a time when conservatism came back into favor, the coming liberal reaction will probably cause a return to 1960s music, most probably a folk-oriented type without extensive electrification. That in turn will probably expand, involve increased amplification and technology, and in turn fade away.

In essence, our theory is that rock will fluctuate between poles represented by the 1950s and the 1960s. Of course, the message will always be contemporary, and we would have a hard time predicting what that would be, but it will probably be based on the perception of the 1950s as the conservative pole and the 1960s as the liberal pole. Therefore, our final conclusion is that rock will have as its main elements the musical framework of the first two decades of its formal existence and that societal views will be expressed within that basic framework.

CHAPTER FIFTEEN

Rock Hall of Fame

After reading about rock and roll and living with it for years, I have seen some musicians emerge as obvious leaders. This listing is of course subjective, and I suggest that the reader form his or her own list, realizing that it will probably change over time as individual biases change. This listing is historical and looks backward in time. The leaders of the 1980s will be listed when history has had time to decide just who they were.

Gregg Allman: One of the Allman Brothers, who has been the mainstay of the Allman Brothers Band; his brother Duane died in a motorcycle accident in 1973. Gregg has a powerful stage presence and has been a model for Southern blues-based rock.

The Beatles: Each of the four members of the Beatles could be cited in this chapter for their individual contribution to the art form. However, as a group they overshadowed every other group in the 1960s and had a lasting influence on later musicians. They were important both because of their artistic achievement and their financial success, serving as a marketing model for groups to follow.

Chuck Berry: One of the most influential guitar players of all time, Berry is still a vibrant performer of rock and roll. Although most at home in the style of the 1950s, he has changed over time to include at least more current lyrics. Berry is often mentioned by later musicians as having been an early influence on them.

Moody Blues: Started in 1964, this English group is important in the sense that they were early experimenters in full orchestration and electronic effects. They have also been quite successful in selling records and providing an alternative art form.

David Bowie: An extremely energetic and theatrical performer, Bowie was the leader of the punk movement long before it actually began. His support of other musicians, in particular Iggy Pop, and his creative daring warrant his place on this list.

Doobie Brothers: Often called the West Coast version of the Allman Brothers, the Doobies were a blues or boogie-woogie based band which enjoyed tremendous success in the early to mid-1970s. They are important because they were a logical extension of the San Francisco sound (a la Moby Grape).

James Brown: As the King of Soul, Brown has been a powerful leader both personally and musically. His singing style is very strong and he has been an influential leader in black rock. The fact that he has crossover popularity speaks to his talent, and his clear influence on funk makes him significant.

Ray Charles: As a seasoned veteran by the time he started making hits, Charles was probably responsible for legitimizing rock in the late 1950s, especially with his combination of jazz, gospel, blues, and rock. He began the jazz-rock movement and popularized the electric piano. A gifted musician, he brought together outstanding musicians and contributed to the art of studio recording.

Justin Hayward of the Moody Blues *(Photo by Barry Rankin)*

Eric Clapton: Clapton played with four important groups early in his career — the Yardbirds, Cream, Derek and the Dominoes, and Blind Faith. With backup groups and as a soloist, Clapton is a virtuoso guitar player. A steady influence on other musicians, he added immeasurably to the standard of technical guitar playing, plus playing some of the most driving and excellent rock music.

George Clinton: Clinton is acknowledged as the purist of funk, being the leader of the Funkadelic/Parliament combination. He developed his musical groups from mainstream soul to free-form funk in the early 1970s and has consistently stood for funk as a relatively pure black art form. He has been critical of other groups, such as Earth, Wind and Fire, because of his deep beliefs.

David Bowie *(Courtesy of RCA Records)*

David Bowie *(Courtesy of RCA Records)*

Alice Cooper: Born Vincent Furnier, Alice Cooper has been a leader in the bizarre circle of rock. If theatricality has been significant in rock, Cooper has certainly paved the way for groups like Kiss and numerous other punk groups.

David Bowie *(Courtesy of RCA Records)*

The Doobie Brothers in concert, 1979 *(Photo by Barry Rankin)*

Jim Croce: Although he died in 1973, Jim Croce is still influential in rock song writing. He was a competent guitarist but it was in his song writing that he was most influential. He wrote a number of important tunes, including "Bad, Bad Leroy Brown."

Bob Dylan: Probably the musician most influential on rock lyrics, Dylan was a symbol of the 1960s. He brought in folk music as appropriate subject matter for a rock group. He was most responsible for raising the political consciousness of rock groups, and he has had lasting influence on many rock musicians from the mid-1960s to the present.

Keith Emerson: Emerson, Lake, and Palmer was a fascinating group which combined the virtuosic abilities of Emerson on keyboard instruments with a rather bizarre attitude toward theatricality. They used numerous electronic effects well and were very popular in the early 1970s. The subject matter of their music was at times quite distant from traditional rock, even including a version of Modest Mussorgsky's *Pictures at an Exhibition.*

John Entwistle: Entwistle is the tall and quiet bass player for the Who. There should be room in this chapter for the guy who holds together a bunch of maniacs, and that is usually the bass player. Besides that, Entwistle is a very competent musician and played a very major role in a group which was dynamically versatile.

Aretha Franklin: One of the real queens of soul music, Franklin was first a gospel singer and then broadened her style to include the blues. She has been enormously successful in both sacred and secular music, and her strong emotional voice is truly both great and distinctive.

Jerry Garcia: Garcia is the long-time leader of the Grateful Dead and is the prototypical hippie musician, although he is now over 40. Garcia has lived his cause for a long time and he is an excellent technician.

Jimi Hendrix: Hendrix was probably the best guitar player, from a technical point of view, from the United States, at least in rhythm and blues and rock. His performances (1966 to 1970) were awe-inspiring if for no other reason than the tremendous number of notes he was capable of playing in such a short period of time. Hendrix influenced many musicians, including white musicians, in sheer technique. This influence was relatively unusual for a black musician, other examples being Charlie Parker, Stanley Clarke, and Herbie Hancock.

Buddy Holly: Holly was very significant in the 1950s and probably would have continued as a significant musician had he not died. However, the legend of Buddy Holly lives on as a symbol for what the rock star is. Although his memory may be more important than his contribution, that is reason enough to include him.

Mick Jagger: As the leader of the Rolling Stones, Jagger established himself as a major singer of rock. His technique was strong and his image clear. His consistency over time has made him highly significant to the development of the form.

Elton John: As a song writer in combination with Bernie Taupin, John was the most important musician of the mid-1970s, as indicated by his earnings. However, John is most significant because he changed the melodic character of rock tunes; he is also an excellent pianist.

Janis Joplin: Joplin was a powerful female singer, and with Big Brother and the Holding Company, she showed conclusively that a woman could be a successful lead singer. Although she died from drugs, Joplin began a tradition of female lead singers with rock bands.

B. B. King: King was an early influence on rock and roll musicians, and he has remained the "king" of the blues. His vitality in singing had lasting impact on many other musicians, including some from this list of major artists, although he was not an extremely good guitarist.

Kiss: Kiss set the standard for theatricality in rock. Although not usually categorized as a punk group, Kiss certainly provided some of the typical stage techniques and as a hard rock band they were quite competent.

Gladys Knight: Knight was very successful within the soul market but she also has great crossover popularity. Her soul music is a soft form of the style and is pop-oriented, but Gladys Knight and the Pips are good performers and are excellent models for a very popular style.

Florence LaRue: The very beautiful lead singer of the Fifth Dimension, LaRue's style has not changed much over the years but it has proven to be a successful model. The Fifth Dimension is a folk group of the 1960s but continues to have great popularity even today. Their style is soft rock and is basically soul-oriented; however, it has great crossover popularity.

John McLaughlin: Sometimes not considered a rock musician at all, McLaughlin has performed rock even though his music usually transcends any one style. He is clearly the most virtuosic guitar player of the twentieth century.

Jim Morrison: Morrison, of the Doors, was very significant in the late 1960s and early 1970s, first because the Doors was an underground group in Los Angeles (when Los Angeles was not supposed to have that kind of thing), but also because he was a strong and effective singer who foreshadowed what singers would do in the 1970s. Morrison had a theatrical background and his artistic productions became total theater. He died in 1971.

Ted Nugent: A guitarist from Detroit, Nugent started out as an animalistic guitar player, both in style and technique, and he never lost that image. A protopunker, Nugent assaults his audience, but unlike some of the mainstream punk musicians he does it with considerable talent.

Elvis Presley: Presley was a phenomenal singer and a performer of major proportions. On top of his talent, he was the model for correct marketing. He was called the "king" of rock for many reasons, and at least one of them was that he was the most financially successful of all the rock stars.

The Ramones: Their image is significant, having turned rock and roll into a spectacle and a means by which to laugh at the world. In this area they certainly succeeded.

Little Richard: Little Richard was the classic rock screamer and he did it better than anyone to date. Although he was most important in the late 1950s, the image of him letting loose will remain with rock forever.

Linda Ronstadt: Ronstadt was a significant part of the West Coast scene starting in the late 1960s. She sings in a light or country rock style and is a good example of the continued importance of female folk-rock musicians.

Florence LaRue of the Fifth Dimension *(Courtesy of the Sterling/Winters Company)*

Linda Ronstadt *(Photo by Barry Rankin)*

Johnny Rotten: Rotten is the kind of guy that one includes reluctantly because he is not very likeable. However, Rotten and his sidekick Sid Vicious were very important images of punk rock. Their names tell it all but they were true to their philosophy; therefore, they were important symbols.

Bob Seger: Seger is one of those musicians who has been very popular and successful without getting much publicity. However, his Silver Bullet Band hit it big in 1976 and has remained powerful ever since. Seger does not fit into any of the types of late 1970s rock — punk, new wave, fusion, or others. He simply plays excellent music with enormous success, both as a singer and as a guitarist.

Wayne Shorter: Saxophonist with Weather Report, Shorter has been responsible for raising the standard of rock playing. Weather Report is both a jazz and a rock group and the instrumental playing of Shorter has influenced other players into searching for more creative ideas.

Grace Slick: Like Janis Joplin, Slick was significant because she was female and the leader of a hard rock band. Although the Airplane and the Starship were San Francisco rock bands, Slick transcended that image because she had such strength.

Bruce Springsteen: In the late 1970s, Springsteen was being touted as the new Dylan. He is a powerful performer, and his lyrics are poetically complex. Although it is perhaps too early to tell, Springsteen may well be the major artist to emerge from that decade.

Pete Townshend: The lead guitarist of the Who, Townshend is a very technical player and quite innovative. Besides the fact that the Who is very successful, Townshend in particular combines both bizarre stage antics with excellent guitar playing.

Dionne Warwick: One of the classiest pop, show, and soul singers of the last two decades, Warwick sets a standard for performance. She has excellent command of her voice and a very appealing personality.

Brian Wilson: Wilson is tremendously important to rock, although not as a musician or lyricist. His importance is in capturing a sound and carrying it through. The Beach Boys developed a truly unique concept in rock, and Wilson was the entire creative force behind it. It was optimistic music, perhaps even a bit out of touch, but it spoke very clearly to people who liked it. Wilson deserves credit for his tenacity, for his continued creativity, and for his success in communication.

Stevie Wonder: Clearly one of the most successful black singers of the 1970s, Wonder has a versatile style which allows him to move freely through different styles of music. He is also the most highly paid rock musician in the world.

Frank Zappa: Although not a commercial success, Zappa is the esoteric intellectual's rock musician. Never to be pinned down, Zappa gives more than most people understand.

Bob Seger in 1977 *(Photo by Barry Rankin)*

Josef Zawinul: Like Wayne Shorter, Zawinul played with Miles Davis prior to joining Weather Report. His background is interesting in that he is Viennese and received his piano training in Europe. Zawinul is a model for the highly trained rock musician of the 1970s.

Led Zeppelin: This group was sometimes overshadowed by other British groups, which is probably unfair. Led Zeppelin was enormously successful for a number of years, for both technical and marketing reasons. They were a very versatile band, combining influences from many different types of music.

CONCLUSION

Obviously, the history of rock is not over. However, we have established some basic premises, with which we will conclude:

1. Rock is a legitimate art form, with its own technique and its own complexity.
2. Like any art form, it has its highs and lows. However, whenever things seemed static, someone has come along to breathe vitality into the tired body.
3. We can trace cycles in rock, which seem to correlate with societal views.
4. Rock has had a major influence on society and on other art forms. This is perhaps the best proof of its effectiveness as an art form.
5. Although it began as a way for youth to rebel against their parents, rock is now a universal art form and a means of communication, spanning the gamut of generations all over the world.

DISCOGRAPHY

This selected discography lists albums that were available as of summer 1981. Anyone seeking additional records by the groups mentioned in this book should consult a *Schwann Catalog*, available at local record stores.

Chapters One and Two

Black Swing Tradition	2-Savoy 2246
Boogie Woogie Rarities (1927-1943)	Mile. 2009
Copulatin' Blues	Stash 101
From Spirituals to Swing	2-Van. T. 47/48
Gut Bucket Blues and Stomps	Her. 112
History of Rhythm and Blues, Vols. 1-8	Atlantic SD8161, 8162, 8163, 8164, 8193, 8194, 8208, 8209
Jazz—Vols. 1-11	Folk. 2801-2811
Oldies but Goodies, Vols. 1-10	OSR-LPS 8850, 8852-8860
Piano Ragtimes, Vols. 1-3	Her. 402, 405, 406
Smithsonian Collection of Classic Jazz	Col. P611891

Chapter Three

Haley, Bill
Golden Hits	2-MCA 4010
Greatest Hits	MCA 161E
Rock and Roll Revival	Pick 3280

Chapter Four

Elvis Aaron Presley (1955-1980)	8-RCA CPL8-3699

Chapter Five

Anka, Paul
Lonely Boy	Pick 3523
21 Golden Hits	RCA AYL1-3808

Avalon, Frankie
Venus	De-lite 2020

Berry, Chuck
Golden Hits	Mer. 61103
Greatest Hits	Arc. Folk 321

Boone, Pat
16 Great Performances	MCA AB-4006

Checker, Chubby
Greatest Hits	2-Abkco 4219

Cooke, Sam
Best	RCA ANL1-3466
2 Sides of Sam Cooke	Spec. 2119E

Curtis, King
Best	Prest. 7709
Soul Meeting	Prest. 7833

Diddley, Bo
Two Great Guitars	Checker 2991

Dion and the Belmonts
Greatest Hits	Col. C-31942

Domino, Fats
Fats Domino	Arc. Folk 280

Eddy, Duane
Have Twangy Guitar	Jamie 3000
Pure Gold	RCA ANL1-2671

Holly, Buddy
Rock 'n Roll Collection	2-MCA 4009E
20 Golden Greats	MCA 3040

Lewis, Jerry Lee
  Golden Rock and Roll   Sun 1000
  Memories   Mer. 5004
Little Richard
  Fabulous Little
    Richard   Spec. 2104
Nelson, Ricky
  Playing to Win   Cap. S00-12109
  Ricky   U Artists LM-1004
Various Artists
  At the Hop   MCA DXS 528
  Rock Begins, Vols. 1
    and 2   Atco SD 33-314 and 315
  The Rock and Roll
    Stars   Buddah BDS 7503

Chapter Six

Agnew, Spiro
  2 Attacks on TV
    and Press   Lava STA-235
Kennedy, John F.
  Inaugural Address   Sp. Arts 1034
King, Jr., Martin Luther
  Free At Last   Gor. 7-929
  Great March on
    Washington   Gor. 7-908
  Great March to
    Freedom   Gor. 7-906
  In Search of Freedom   Mer. 61170
McCarthy,
  Sen. Joseph R.   Folk 5450
Nixon, Richard M.
  Checkers Speech   Lava RMN-235
Un-American Activities
  Committee   Folk 5530

Chapter Seven

Beatles
  Abbey Road   Cap. SO-383
  Early Beatles   Cap. ST-2309
  1962–1966   2-Cap. SKBO-3403
  1966–1970   2-Cap. SKBO-3404
  Revolver   Cap. SW-2576
  Rubber Soul   Cap. SW-2442
  Yellow Submarine   Cap. SW-153

Chapter Eight

Beach Boys
  Dance, Dance, Dance   Cap. SN-16019
  Fun, Fun, Fun   Cap. SN-16018
  Good Vibrations   Reprise 2280
  Surf's Up   Reprise 6453
Big Brother and the
  Holding Company
  Cheap Thrills   Col. PC-9700
Grateful Dead
  Anthem of the Sun   War. 1749
  Grateful Dead   War. 1689
Jan and Dean
  Legendary Masters,
    No. 3   2-U Artists 9961

Jefferson Airplane
  Bless Its Pointed
    Little Head   RCA AYL1-3799
  Surrealistic Pillow   RCA-AYL1-3738
Moby Grape
  Great Grape   Col. C31098
  Wow/Grape Jams   2-Col. CXS3

Chapter Ten

Mahavishnu Orchestra
  Birds of Fire   Col. PC-31996
Stevie Wonder
  Songs in the Key
    of Life   2-Tam. 13-340C2
Weather Report
  Heavy Weather   Col. PC-34418

Chapter Eleven

John, Elton
  Capt. Fantastic and
    the Brown Dirt
    Cowboy   MCA 3009
  Don't Shoot Me...   MCA 3005
  Empty Sky   MCA 3008
  Madman Across the
    Water   MCA 3003
  Single Man   MCA 3065
  Tumbleweed
    Connection   MCA 3001
  Yellow Brick Road   2-MCA 3001
Rolling Stones
  At Their Satanic
    Majesties' Request   Lon. NPS-2(7)
  Beggar's Banquet   Lon. 539(7)
  Get Yer Ya-Ya's Out   Lon. NPS-5(7)
  Goat's Head Soup   Rol. 39106
  It's Only Rock and
    Roll   Rol. 79101
  Out of Our Heads   Lon. 429(7)
  Sticky Fingers   Rol. 59100
The Who
  Magic Bus/My
    Generation   2-MCA 4068
  Meaty, Beaty, Big and
    Bouncy   MCA 3025
  Quadrophenia   2-MCA 10004
  Tommy   2-MCA 10005
  Who Are You?   MCA 3050

Chapter Twelve

Captain Beefheart and
  His Magic Band
  Shiny Beast   War. 3256
  Trout Mask Replica   2-Reprise 2027
Crosby, Stills, Nash and
  Young
  Crosby, Stills and
    Nash   At. 19104
  Deja Vu   At. 19118
  Four Way Street   2-At. 2-902

Dylan, Bob
  Bob Dylan — Col. PC-8579
  Self Portrait — 2-Col. P2X-30050
  Times They Are A-Changin' — Col. PC-8905

Dylan, Bob, with the Band
  Basement Tapes — 2-Col. C2-33682

Fifth Dimension
  Up, Up and Away — Lib. SCM 91000

Fugs
  Golden Filth — Reprise 6396

Mothers of Invention
  Fillmore East — Reprise 2042
  Joe's Garage — Zappa 1603
  Joe's Garage Acts II and III — 2-Zappa 1502
  Ruben and the Jets
  Uncle Meat — 2-Reprise 2Ms-2024

Peter, Paul and Mary
  Peter, Paul and Mary — War. 1449
  Peter, Paul and Mommy — War. 1785
  Reunion — War. 3231

Chapter Thirteen

Blood, Sweat and Tears
  Blood, Sweat and Tears — Col. PC-9720
  Child Is Father to the Man — Col. PC-9619

Brown, James
  Original Disco Man — Pol. 6212
  Take a Look At — Pol. 6181

Chicago
  Chicago Transit Authority — 2-Col. PG-8
  Chicago III — 2-Col. C2-30110
  Chicago V — Col. PC-31102
  Chicago X — Col. PC-34200

Clarke, Stanley
  Children of Forever (with Chick Corea) — Pol. 5531
  School Days — Col. PE-36975
  Stanley Clarke — Col. PE-36973

Cobham, Billy
  Crosswinds — At. 7300
  Spectrum — At. 7268

Commodores
  Heroes — Mo. 8-939
  Midnight Magic — Mo. 8-926

Corea, Chick
  Chick Corea — 2-Blue LA395-H
  Inner Space — 2-At. 2-305
  Spanish Heart — 2-Pol. 9003

Earth, Wind and Fire
  Head — Col. PC-32194
  Need of Love — War. 1958
  Way of the World — Col. PC-33280

Electric Flag
  Long Time Comin' — Col. CS-9597

Emerson, Lake and Palmer
  Brain Salad Surgery — At. 19124
  Emerson, Lake and Palmer — At. 19120
  Pictures at an Exhibition — At. 19122
  Trilogy — At. 19123
  Welcome Back — 3-Mant. 200

Funkadelics
  Electric Spanking of Babies — War. 3482
  Uncle Jam Wants You — War. HS-3371

Hancock, Herbie
  An Evening with Chick Corea — 2-Col. PG-34688
  Sextent — Col. C-32212
  V.S.O.P. — 2-Col. PG-34688

Kool and the Gang
  Celebrate — De-Lite 9518

Mahavishnu Orchestra (John McLaughlin)
  Birds of Fire — Col. PC-31996
  Bitches Brew (Miles Davis) — 2-Col. PG-26

Parliament
  Gloryhallastoopid — Casa. 7195

Ponty, Jean-Luc
  Cosmic Messenger — At. 19189
  A Taste for Passion — At. 19253

Santana
  Abraxas — Col. JC-30130
  Caravanserai — Col. PC-31619
  Santana — Col. PC-9781

Summer, Donna
  Bad Girls — 2-Casa. 7150
  Love Trilogy — Casa. 5004N
  Walk Away — Casa. 7244

Weather Report (See Chapter Ten)

Chapter Fourteen

AC/DC
  Dirty Deeds — At. 16033

Adam and the Ants
  Kings of the Wild Frontier — Epic JE-37033

B-52's
  The B-52's — War. 3355
  Wild Planet — War. 3471

Blondie
  Eat to the Beat — Chrys. CHE-1225

Bowie, David
  Scary Monsters — RCA AQL1-3647

Buzzcocks
  A Different Kind of Tension — A & M SP-009

Clash
  Give 'Em Enough Rope — Epic JE-35543
  Sandinista — 3-Epic E3X-37037

Costello, Elvis
   Taking Liberties — Col. JC-36839
Iggy and the Stooges
   Raw Power — Col. PC-32111
Knack
   ... but the Little Girls Understand — Cap. S00-12145
   Get the Knack — Cap. S0-11948
Parker, Graham
   Squeezing Out Sparks — Ari. 4223
Plimsouls
   Plimsouls — Planet 13

Pop, Iggy
   New Values — Ari. 4237
   Soldier — Ari. 4259
Sex Pistols
   Never Mind the Bullocks — War. K-3147
Surf Punks
   My Beach — Epic JE-36500
Talking Heads
   Fear of Music — Sire 6076

BIBLIOGRAPHY

BEETHOVEN, JAN, AND CARMAN MOORE. *Rock-It*. Sherman Oaks, Cal.: Alfred Publishing Co., 1980.
BELZ, CARL. *The Story of Rock*, 2nd ed. New York: Oxford University Press, 1972.
BIRD, BRIAN. *Skiffle*. London: Robert Hale Ltd., 1958.
BROWN, CHARLES T. *Proceedings of NAJE, Vol. 1*. Manhattan, Kan.: NAJE Press, 1981.
CHARLES, RAY, AND DAVID RITZ. *Brother Ray*. New York: Dial Press, 1966.
CHRISTGAU, ROBERT. *Any Old Way You Choose It: Rock and Other Pop Music (1967-1973)*. New York: Penguin Books, 1973.
COHN, NIK. *Rock from the Beginning*. New York: Pocket Books, 1969.
_____. *WopBopa LooBop LopBamBoom*. London: Paladin, 1970.
COON, CAROLINE. *1988: The New Wave Punk Rock Explosion*. New York: Hawthorn, 1978.
DAVIES, HUNTER. *The Beatles*. New York: McGraw-Hill, 1968.
DENISOFF, R. SERGE, AND RICHARD A. PETERSON, EDS. *The Sounds of Social Change*. Chicago: Rand McNally, 1972.
DIXON, ROBERT, AND JOHN GODRICH. *Recording the Blues*. New York: Stein and Day, 1970.
EISEN, JONATHAN, ED. *The Age of Rock*. New York: Random House, 1969.
_____. *The Age of Rock 2*. New York: Random House, 1970.
FRITH, SIMON. *The Sociology of Rock*. London: Constable, 1978.
GABREE, JOHN. *The World of Rock*. Greenwich, Conn.: Fawcett Publications, 1968.
GILLETT, CHARLIE. *The Sound of the City—The Rise of Rock and Roll*. New York: Outerbridge and Dienstfrey, 1970.
GLEASON, RALPH J. *The Jefferson Airplane and the San Francisco Sound*. New York: Ballantine, 1969.
GOLDROSEN, JON. *Buddy Holly: His Life and Music*. Bowling Green, Ohio: Bowling Green University Press, 1975.
HOPKINS, JERRY. *Elvis*. New York: Simon and Schuster, 1971.
_____. *The Rock Story*. New York: New American Library, 1970.
JONES, LEROI. *Blues People*. New York: William Morrow, 1967.
KEIL, CHARLES. *Urban Blues*. Chicago: University of Chicago Press, 1966.
LEAF, DAVID. *The Beach Boys and the California Myth*. New York: Grosset & Dunlap, 1978.
LOGAN, NICK, AND BOB WOFFINDEN. *The Illustrated Encyclopedia of Rock*. New York: Harmony Books, 1977.

MARCUS, GREIL. *Mystery Train.* New York: Dutton and Co., 1976.
MELLERS, WILFRED. *Twilight of the Gods: The Beatles in Retrospect.* New York: Viking Press, 1974.
MILLER, JIM, ED. *The Rolling Stone Illustrated History of Rock and Roll.* New York: Random House, 1980.
ORLOFF, KATHERINE. *Rock 'n Roll Woman.* Los Angeles: Nash Publishing, 1974.
PREISS, BYRON. *The Beach Boys.* New York: Ballantine, 1979.
The Rolling Stone Interviews. New York: Straight Arrow Publishers, 1971.
ROWE, MIKE. *Chicago Breakdown.* New York: Drake Publishers, 1975.
ROXON, LILLIAN. *Rock Encyclopedia.* New York: Grosset & Dunlap, 1969.
SCADUTO, ANTHONY. *Bob Dylan: An Intimate Biography.* New York: Grosset & Dunlap, 1971.
———. *The Beatles.* New York: New American Library, 1968.
———. *Schwann Record and Tape Guide.* Boston: ABC Schwann Publications, 1981.
WENNER, JANN, ED. *Rolling Stone* (magazine). New York: Straight Arrow Publishers.

INDEX

ABBA, 119
Adam and the Ants, 171, 172, 180
Africans. *See* Slave music
Afro-Americans. *See* Slave music
Allman Brothers, 183
Amplifiers. *See* Electronic devices
Andrews Sisters, 25, 56
Anka, Paul, 57, 66
Ars antiqua, 174
Ars nova, 174
Attitudes
   1950s, capsule view, 20–22
      communism, 21, 22
      financial, 21
      politics, 20–21
   1960s, 78–80
      change, 78
      civil rights, 79
      heroes, 79–80
      Kent State, 79
      politics, 78–79
   1970s, 109–11
Autry, Gene, 56
Avalon, Frankie, 57, 66

B-52's, 173
Baez, Joan, 133, 144
Ballard, Hank, 71
Baraka, Imamu Amirir. *See* Jones, LeRoi
Beach Boys, 29, 42, 47, 49, 97–102, 107, 193
Beat, 176
Beatles, 26, 29, 30, 39, 47, 49, 57, 69, 72, 78, 81–94, 96, 119, 120, 121, 123, 126, 142, 148, 183
BeeGees, 162
Bennett, Tony, 56
Benson, George, 149, 156
Berry, Chuck, 27, 52, 53, 54, 58–59, 98, 149, 183
Best, Pete, 83–84
Big Bopper, 62, 71
Big Brother and the Holding Company, 104, 105, 189
Black, Bill, 37
Black Sabbath, 107
Blasters, 180
Blind Faith, 184
Blitz, 180
Blondie, 105, 173, 174
Blood, Sweat and Tears, 104, 143, 149
Blues, 9–13
Bo Diddley, 58, 61
Boone, Pat, 66, 68
Bowie, David, 183, 185, 186
Broonzy, Bill, 11
Brown, James, 150, 161, 162, 183
Bubble gum music, 68
Buffalo Springfield, 142–43
Butterfield Blues Band, 135
Buzzcocks, 176
Byrds, 142

Cale, John, 170
Call and response. *See* Slave music
Callers. *See* Slave music
Captain Beefheart, 145
Carson, Rachel, 79
Carter, Jimmy, 109
Cash, Johnny, 36
Chants. *See* Slave music
Charles, Ray, 54, 57, 72–75, 138, 148, 149, 183
Checker, Chubby, 57, 71
Chicago, 149–50
Chipmunks, 54
Chordettes, 57
Civil rights. *See* Attitudes
Clapton, Eric, 184
Clark, Gene, 142
Clarke, Stanley, 150, 161, 189
Clash, 177, 179
Clinton, George, 171, 176, 184
Clooney, Rosemary, 56
Coasters, 71
Cobham, Bill, 150
Cole, Nat King, 13, 18, 56
Coleman, Ornette, 180
Collins, Judy, 135
Coltrane, Alice, 168
Coltrane, John, 17, 61, 168
Comets. *See* Haley, Bill
Commodores, 161
Communism. *See* Attitudes
Como, Perry, 56
Cooke, Sam, 58, 61
Cooper, Alice, 186
Corea, Chick, 149, 150, 156, 168
Costello, Elvis, 176
Count Basie, 8, 75
Cream, 184
Creech, Papa John, 156

Crewcuts, 57
Croce, Jim, 188
Crosby, Bing, 18
Crosby, David, 142–44
Crosby, Stills, Nash and Young, 142–44
Crudup, Arthur, 37
Cry. *See* Slave music

Damned, 171
Davis, Miles, 150, 152, 156, 195
Day, Doris, 57
Devo, 173
Dion and the Belmonts, 66, 68
Disco, 48, 129, 162, 168
Domino, Fats, 17, 49, 52, 68, 91
Donnegan, Lonnie, 83
Doobie Brothers, 183
Doors, 102, 190
Dorsey Brothers, 49
Duke, George, 146
Dyke and the Blazers, 160
Dylan, Bob, 102, 133, 135, 188

Earth, Wind and Fire, 151–52, 161, 184
Eddy, Duane, 62, 115
Electric Flag, 104, 152
Electronic devices, 113–17
 amplifiers, 113–14
 microphones, 48, 113–14
 speakers, 114
 synthesizers, 115–16
Ellington, Duke, 7–8
Elliot, Cass, 140
Emerson, Lake and Palmer, 152, 188
Epstein, Brian, 84, 92
Extramusical effects, 116

Fabian, 66, 68–69
Fabulous Thunderbirds, 180
Faces, 123
Ferguson, Maynard, 129, 156
Field holler. *See* Slave music
Fifth Dimension, 138, 190
Fisher, Eddie, 57
Fitzgerald, Ella, 11
Flock of Seagulls, 180
Flying Burrito Brothers, 142
Folk-rock, 132–44
Ford, Tennessee Ernie, 57
Four Freshmen, 98
Franklin, Aretha, 17, 189
Freed, Alan, 22
Fugs, 145, 170
Funk, 48, 148, 160–61
Funkadelics, 161

Gang of Four, 176
Gant, Cecil, 18

Garcia, Jerry, 105–6, 189
Goodman, Benny, 13
Gospel. *See* Slave music
Grateful Dead, 105–6, 189
Guthrie, Arlo, 133
Guthrie, Woody, 133

Haight-Ashbury, 103
Haley, Bill, 17, 25–30, 33, 42, 49, 52, 54, 57, 58, 64, 68, 121
Hampton, Lionel, 13, 17
Hancock, Herbie, 149, 152, 156
Harrison, George. *See* Beatles
Hendrix, Jimi, 105, 170, 189
Heroes. *See* Attitudes
Holliday, Billie, 11, 13
Hollies, 143
Holly, Buddy, 61, 62, 71, 122, 189
Hopkins, Lightnin', 11
Hunter, Ivory Joe, 17, 25
Hunter, Tab, 57

Jackson Five, 161
Jagger, Mick, 49, 86, 171, 189
Jan and Dean, 98
Jefferson Airplane (Starship), 104, 193
John, Elton, 127–29, 189
Johnson, James, 7
Johnson, Lyndon, 79
Jones, LeRoi, 2
Jones, Spike, 29
Jones, Tom, 49
Joplin, Janis, 104, 189
Jordan, Louis, 17, 25, 75

Kennedy, John F., 78, 79
Kent State. *See* Attitudes
King, B. B., 11, 189
King Curtis, 17, 58, 61
Kingston Trio, 133
Kiss, 107, 116, 186, 190
Knight, Gladys, 190
Kool and the Gang, 161
Kooper, Al, 104, 149
Kraftwerk, 180

LaRue, Florence, 190
Leadbelly, 11, 17
Led Zeppelin, 129, 195
Lennon, John. *See* Beatles
Lewis, Jerry Lee, 36, 62–63
Little Richard, 17, 26, 54, 63–64, 84, 89, 105, 190
Loa. *See* Slave music
Lomax, Alan, 133
Lovin' Spoonful, 138, 140

Madness, 176
Magazine, 176
Magic Band, 145
Mahavishnu Orchestra, 156, 190

Mamas and the Papas, 140
Mangione, Chuck, 162
Mann, Herbie, 150
Martin, Dean, 18, 57
Martin, Dewey, 143
Martin, George, 84, 92
Material, 180
Materialism. *See* Attitudes
MC5, 145, 170
McCartney, Paul. *See* Beatles
McGhee, Stick, 19
McGuinn, Roger, 142
McLaren, Malcolm, 173
Men at Work, 180
Messina, Jim, 143
Microphones. *See* Electronic devices
Miller, Glenn, 18–19, 71–72
Mills Brothers, 25
Mitchell, Joni, 133, 135, 149
Moby Grape, 104
Mod, 124
Monkees, 49, 145, 171
Monroe, Bill, 37
Moody Blues, 183
Moore, Scotty, 37
Morrison, Jim, 102, 190
Morton, Jelly Roll, 8
Mothers of Invention. *See* Zappa, Frank
Motown, 52, 72, 160
Muzak, 162

Nader, Ralph, 79
Nash, Graham, 143–44
Neal, Bob, 37
Nelson, Ricky, 66, 69
New Riders of the Purple Sage, 142
New wave, 174–80
 Ska, 176
New York Dolls, 173
Nixon, Richard, 78, 79, 109
Nugent, Ted, 190

Ono, Yoko, 86
Opera, 125–26

Page, Patti, 56
Parker, Charlie, 17, 189
Parker, "Colonel" Tom, 37, 38, 49
Parker, Graham, 176
Parks, Van Dyke, 100
Parliament, 161
Partridge Family, 69
Peter, Paul and Mary, 135
Peterson, Oscar, 7
Phillips, Dewey, 37
Phillips, Sam, 36–37
Pickett, Boris, 57, 72
Poco, 143

Politics. *See* Attitudes
Pompanelli, Rudy, 17
Ponty, Jean-Luc, 156
Pop, Iggy, 170–71, 183
Presley, Elvis, 17, 23, 25, 29, 30, 33–50, 52, 54, 55, 57, 58, 62, 63, 65, 68, 69, 85, 89, 94, 98, 121, 170, 190
Progressions. *See* Blues
Protestant hymn. *See* Slave music
Punk, 102, 170–73

Quarrymen. *See* Beatles

Race records, 13–14
Rainey, Ma, 11
Ramones, 173, 190
Rap, 161
Ravens, 23, 55
Ray, Johnnie, 17, 56
Reagan, Ronald, 110
Richardson, J. P. *See* Big Bopper
Rockabilly, 14
Rollins, Sonny, 17
Ronstadt, Linda, 190
Roosevelt, Franklin, 78
Ross, Diana, 162
Rotten, Johnny, 171, 193
Rural and urban. *See* Blues

Sanders, Ed, 145
Sands, Tommy, 66, 69
Santana, Carlos, 156
Seals and Crofts, 140–41
Sebastian, John, 138, 140
Seeger, Charles, 133
Seeger, Pete, 133, 146

Seger, Bob, 193, 194
Selector, 176
Sex Pistols, 171
Sha-Na-Na, 29
Shaw, Arnold, 11–12
Shaw, Arty, 13
Shorter, Wayne, 156, 193, 195
Simon and Garfunkel, 142
Sinatra, Frank, 13, 18, 55
Sinatra, Nancy, 62, 69
Ska. *See* New wave
Skiffle, 82, 83, 84
Slave music, 2–6
Slick, Grace, 104, 193
Smith, Bessie, 11
Smith, Kate, 162
Smith, Willie "The Lion," 7
Social reflection. *See* Attitudes
Soft-Cell, 180
Soul, 129, 160–61
Speakers. *See* Electronic devices
Specials, 176, 177
Springsteen, Bruce, 193
Starlight Wranglers, 37
Starr, Ringo. *See* Beatles
Stiff Little Fingers, 176
Stills, Stephen, 133, 143–44
Stooges, 170–71
Stray Cats, 176, 180
Sullivan, Ed, 49, 85
Summer, Donna, 162, 168
Sun Records, 36
Synthesizers. *See* Electronic devices

Talking Heads, 173, 177, 180
Tatum, Art, 7

Taupin, Bernie, 189
Travolta, John, 162
Turner, Joe, 13, 17

Ultra-Vox, 180
Undertones, 176

Valens, Richie, 62, 71
Vallee, Rudy, 18, 65
Van Vliet, Don, 145
Velvet Underground, 170

Walker, T-Bone, 11
Waller, Thomas "Fats," 7
Warwick, Dionne, 193
Watergate. *See* Attitudes
Waters, Ethel, 11
Weather Report, 156, 193, 195
West Africans. *See* Slave Music
Western swing, 14
Who, 72, 116, 123–26, 130, 170, 189, 193
Wilson, Brian. *See* Beach Boys
Wilson, Teddy, 13
Wings, 87
Wire, 176
Wonder, Stevie, 74, 193
Wooley, Sheb, 72

XTC, 176

Yardbirds, 184
Young, Neil, 142–44

Zappa, Frank, 145–46, 170, 193
Zawinul, Josef, 156, 195